VEGETABLES
THE PRACTICAL GUIDE TO SUCCESS

VEGETABLES
THE PRACTICAL GUIDE TO SUCCESS

BERNARD SALT

B T BATSFORD · LONDON

Published in 2000 by
B.T. Batsford,
9 Blenheim Court,
Brewery Road,
London N7 9NT.

A member of the Chrysalis Group plc

First published in 1995 by Moorland Publishing Co Ltd.

British Library Cataloguing in Publication Data:
A catalogue record for this title is available from the British Library.

Illustrations have been supplied as follows:

Front and back cover, frontispiece and preface: *Garden Answers magazine*
Page 29: Garden Direct.
Page 40: Traditional Garden Supply Co.

ISBN 0 7134 8621 X

Printed in Hong Kong

Contents

PREFACE

Growing vegetables is a key to good health; growers get exercise as well as healthy food. Fresh vegetables not only taste better than purchased ones – they are better. Anyone who claims that supermarket frozen peas taste like garden peas has never eaten fresh garden peas! You may notice that the word 'work' does not appear on these pages; that is because gardening is not work, it is sheer pleasure.

The first section of the book is intended to be read from page 7 through to page 66. The second section lists over 50 vegetables in alphabetical order with specific growing instructions; this section is intended as a reference.

My garden is in the Midlands and consists of badly drained clay soil. It is divided into 2 sections; one is managed traditionally and the other is divided into raised beds. All the photographs were taken in this garden. I also have a polytunnel and this is such a boon to vegetable production that I have included a chapter on its use.

I offer the following advice to all vegetable growers:
• Use the raised bed method of production.
• Whenever possible grow from home-raised transplants.
• Keep chemical sprays to an absolute minimum.

I wish you joy from your vegetable garden and hope that you will give your children a little patch on which to grow their own vegetables. A child who turns up his/her nose at cabbage will have a different attitude when eating one they have grown themselves.

Bernard Salt

1

S O I L

Soil is nature's recycling factory where dead material is broken down into simple non-living salts. These salts are then taken by plant roots to make new living material. The workers in this factory range from large earthworms down to bacteria which are so small that thousands could fit on a pinhead. There are more living things in the soil of an average garden than there are people in the world; there are also many thousands of miles of fine fungus threads – all essential to the life of the soil.

In this country there is a very wide range of soils, there are heavy clays, light sands, acid peats, alkaline chalks and every possible mixture in between. **Gardeners do not choose their soil – they have to manage with the soil they happen to have. However they can manage their soils in such a way that it produces good crops and gradually improves.** An understanding of soil and knowledge of how to manage it is the basis of good gardening.

The bulk of soil is rock that has been ground up into particles over many centuries by the actions of sun, frost, wind and water. Sand is coarsely ground rock – like the sand of the seaside. Clay is finely ground rock – rather like fine flour and intermediate sized particles are called silt. Most soils contain a mixture of all three particles – the amounts of sand, silt and clay however vary, the amount of each determines the soil **texture.**

Soil Type	Percentage of:	Clay	Silt	Sand
Sand		10	10	80
Sandy loam		10	25	65
Loam		20	40	40
Silt loam		20	60	20
Clay loam		40	30	30
Clay		60	20	20

Approximate percentages of clay, silt and sand particles in some soil types.

The texture of a soil (ie the amount of sand, silt and clay present) determines its nature. A clayey soil is sticky when wet and hard when dry; this makes cultivation difficult and is referred to by gardeners as a heavy soil. A sandy soil which is free draining and easy to cultivate is called a **light** soil. Any soil can be made fertile; a **fertile** soil is one which grows a good crop.

In a fertile soil many of the rock particles are bonded into crumbs by organic matter. The crumbs contain many fine pores that hold water; this water is released gradually as fine root hairs extract it. Soil crumbs have spaces in between which allows easy root penetration and the space between them is filled with air – essential for roots to breathe as plants cannot pass oxygen down from the leaves.

The crumbs in a soil are called its **structure.** A layer of crumbs on the surface of a

If work must be done when the soil is wet a plank will help to conserve the soil structure.

These carrots have been grown in badly drained soil

seedlings emerging.

There are several methods of growing plants without soil, growbags or hydroponics (water culture) for example. On a small scale these methods are expensive and can only be justified for the production of high value crops. The basis of vegetable culture is soil.

Soil provides plants with:
- ❏ Physical support.
- ❏ A constant supply of water.
- ❏ A supply of air to the roots.
- ❏ A supply of mineral salts.

Drainage

In some areas the soil is badly drained and in winter the soil may become waterlogged. The water forces air from the soil and plant roots are drowned. In some cases the problem can be helped by double digging, this breaks up the subsoil and allows water to pass through. Double digging will only help if there is somewhere for the water to flow to, a soakaway dug at the lowest point may help.

If the drainage problem cannot be overcome then cropping is possible by the use of raised beds (see page 13). In this situation the beds should be surrounded by boards and some soil imported. Most of the photographs in this book were taken in a garden which has this defect.

Acidity and Alkalinity

Soil is either acid, neutral or alkaline and this is measured on a pH scale. A plant will not thrive if the pH is too high or too low and different plants have different pH requirements. In this country most soils gradually become more acid; this is corrected by the addition of lime. Lime not only increases the pH of the soil it helps clays to form crumbs and it supplies the calcium which plants need in order to grow. Lime increases root growth and earthworm activity, both of which improve the structure of the soil.

well-structured soil is referred to as a **tilth.** Gardeners are not able to alter the texture of their soil but they can maintain and improve its structure. The aim of the vegetable gardener should be to create and conserve a good soil structure. This is obtained by mixing liberal quantities of well-rotted organic material with the soil every year or at least two years out of three. A good soil structure can be destroyed by walking on wet soil or by too much raking.

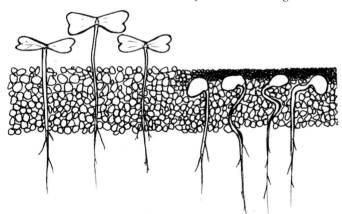

Rain damages soil structure, the soil 'slumps' and a cap forms. Seedlings cannot push through the cap. If this happens, water daily to soften the cap – or cover seeds with compost instead of soil.

Too much raking or heavy rain can break up soil crumbs, when this happens the spaces between the large particles can become blocked by smaller particles and a 'cap' forms. The soil is said to have 'slumped'. A dry cap covers the surface and prevents the passage of air; it also stops

The pH of a soil is easily measured with a kit which is available from garden centres. The pH scale differs from most others, in that a difference of one unit on the scale represents ten. For example a pH of 5.0 is ten times more acid than a pH of 6.0. It is a good idea to test the pH of the soil in the vegetable garden and add lime where necessary. The table shows how much lime to add in order to increase the pH by one unit (eg from 5 to 6).

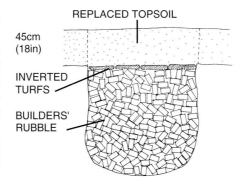

SOIL TYPE	AMOUNT TO ADD
Sandy soil	200g sq m (8oz sq yd)
Loam soil	540g sq m (16oz sq yd)
Clay or peat soil	800g sq m (24oz sq yd)

Lime acts slowly and is best added in the autumn by spreading it on the surface before winter digging. Lime speeds up the breakdown of organic matter and if manure and lime are added together, nitrogen is wasted. One way around this problem is to bury the manure and spread the lime on the surface.

Lime is usually applied every third year to the plot in which brassicas are to be grown. Two types of lime are available, ground limestone and hydrated lime. Ground limestone is slower acting than hydrated lime. Lime is available in the garden centres, if a large quantity is needed a builders' merchant may give better value.

Section through a soakaway. A hole a little more than one metre (39in) deep is dug. The top soil is saved and the subsoil discarded; the hole is then filled with builders' rubble to within 45cm (18in) of the top. The rubble is covered with a layer of inverted turfs and the topsoil is returned

Digging

The first operation in vegetable culture is to dig the soil, the reasons for digging are to:

❑ break up the soil to enable crop plants to form a good rooting system.
❑ leave a bare surface with weeds and remains of the previous crop buried.
❑ remove the roots of perennial weeds eg couch grass and dandelion.
❑ increase the air content of the soil by loosening it up.
❑ add organic material and mix it with the soil.
❑ create the conditions where a tilth can be produced.
❑ expose the soil to frost.

Different plants have different pH requirements

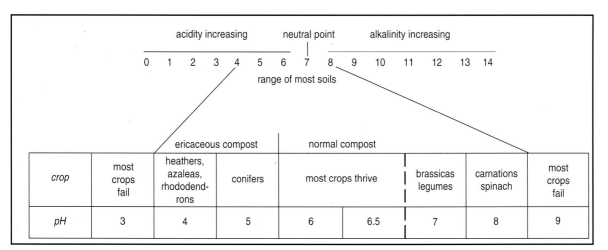

The best time to dig is late autumn, this is not possible with overwintering crops such as leeks and Brussels sprouts, these areas should be dug as soon as possible after the crop has been cleared. When autumn digging, do not chop up the soil into small lumps but leave them the size of a large fist, the action of frost on lumps this size will help to form a better tilth.

Types of Digging

Single spit digging turns over the surface layer to a depth of one spit (ie the length of a spade blade). Digging to a depth of two spits is called **double digging**; a similar effect can be more easily obtained by **bastard trenching.** Any soil that is not free draining should be worked to a depth of two spits every 3 or 4 years. Most soils are best dug in the autumn to allow winter frosts to break up lumps. Soil should not be dug when very wet, to do so may harm the structure.

Single Spit Digging

When adding manure (or other forms of organic waste) spread it from top to bottom over the far side of the trench. This will help to mix the manure with the soil. A layer of organic material should not be dumped in the bottom of a trench as this does little to improve the soil.

Double Digging

This method works the soil to a depth of two spits, assisting drainage and allowing vegetables to form good root systems. Care must be taken to avoid bringing subsoil to the surface. Soils which are not free draining should be worked to this depth every few years.

SOIL FROM A + B   SOIL FROM 1

E	D	C	B	A
5	4	3	2	1

Double digging

❑ Make a trench one spit deep and two spade widths across the end of the plot; this is labelled A and B on the diagram. Barrow the soil from this trench to the far end of the plot.

❑ Make a second trench, in the bottom of the first one, just one spit wide; this is labelled '1' on the diagram. Barrow the soil from this trench to the far end of the plot but keep it separate to the first pile of soil.

❑ Now dig the plot in the following sequence: '2' into '1'; 'C' into 'A'; '3' into '2'; 'D' into 'B' and so on.

❑ When the end of the plot is reached soil from '1' is used to fill the lower trench and soil from 'A' and 'B' is used to fill the wide trench above.

Single spit digging

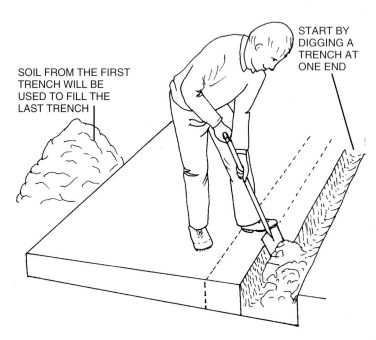

SOIL FROM THE FIRST TRENCH WILL BE USED TO FILL THE LAST TRENCH

START BY DIGGING A TRENCH AT ONE END

Double digging requires considerable skill and should not be attempted until the art of single spit digging has been mastered.

Advantages of Double Digging

Some soils like sands over gravel, chalk and limestone are free draining and are unlikely to benefit from deeper working. Most soils benefit as the hard pan that often forms just under the surface is broken up. Other soils benefit in the following ways:

❏ Improved drainage prevents damage to plant roots by water logging.
❏ The volume of soil which can be easily penetrated by roots is increased; this gives plants an additional supply of water and nutrients.
❏ The hard pan which often forms below the depth of normal cultivations is broken.
❏ Crops grown for their tap roots will be improved.

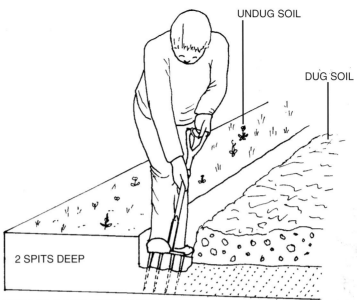

UNDUG SOIL

DUG SOIL

2 SPITS DEEP

THE SOIL IN THE TRENCH BOTTOM IS FORKED AFTER EACH ROW OF DIGGING

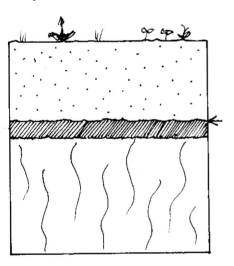

A soil pan is an impervious layer of soil, just below the depth of cultivation. The topsoil above will become waterlogged if the pan is not broken

Preparing a Tilth

After digging, the soil is left untouched for as long as possible. Heavy soils are best left throughout the winter. Frost and rain help to break the surface into a tilth which is suitable for seed sowing.

The garden rake is used to level the surface and break up any large lumps, this is only possible when the lumps are reasonably dry. It is important to use the rake in a forward and back movement, pushing as well as pulling the soil. **Raking should stop as soon as the desired level of tilth is**

Bastard trenching. This is a good alternative to double digging; it is easier, very much quicker and almost as effective

Note the difference good drainage makes to root systems – a plant is only as good as it roots

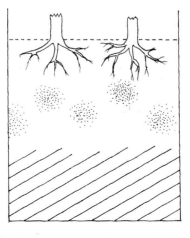

WATERLOGGED SOIL

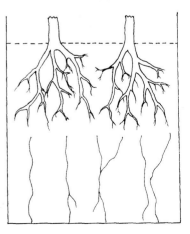

WELL DRAINED SOIL

Raking

❑ Encourages slugs.
❑ Prevents light rain from reaching the soil.
❑ As the mulch decays it forms an ideal place for weed seed germination.

In 'no-dig' systems (possible with some types of well-drained soils in raised beds) manure is not mixed with soil but placed on the surface as a mulch. The activity of earthworms, as they drag the material into their burrows, maintains a good soil structure. Note: The soil must be double-dug before working towards a 'no-dig' system.

Some authorities recommend regular surface hoeing to maintain a mulch of dry soil. Scientific research has failed to find any advantage in doing this. In fact such practice is likely to harm the soil structure.

achieved. This must be fine for sowing small seeds but can be quite coarse for transplanting cabbages or setting potatoes. Too much raking will destroy the structure and lead to a crust through which seedlings cannot push.

The soil is now ready for sowing or planting.

Mulching

A mulch is a layer of material covering the soil. The covering can be inorganic (eg plastic) or organic (eg well-rotted manure). To be effective a layer of organic material should be at least 10cm (4in) thick. Mulching is more common in a flower garden than a vegetable garden although it is the only way to use manure on perennial vegetables such as asparagus and rhubarb.

Mulching has the following advantages:
❑ Protects the soil from heavy rain and stops it from capping.
❑ Suppresses weed seed germination.
❑ Prevents the soil surface from drying out.
❑ Keeps the soil warmer in winter and cooler in summer.
❑ Adds nutrients to the soil.

Mulching has the following disadvantages:

Green Manuring

Growing a leafy crop for the purpose of digging it into the soil is called 'green manuring'. The crop is usually sown in autumn and dug into the soil when it is around 20cm (8in) high in spring. Any hardy crop which germinates and grows away quickly can be used. Mustard and rape are often used as green manures, these are brassicas however and may present disease problems. Grazing rye is the best green manuring crop as it germinates very quickly, withstands the coldest weather and is less likely to attract pigeons than the brassica crops.

The use of green manure reduces the need for nitrogen fertiliser as the crop takes in nitrates during the autumn which would otherwise be washed away with winter rains. The nitrates are released from the decaying crop after it has been dug into the soil. Benefits of green manuring:
❑ Reduces the need for nitrate fertilisers.
❑ Prevents possible pollution by reducing the loss of nitrates from the soil in winter.
❑ Protects the soil surface structure from damage by heavy rain.
❑ Keeps the soil a little drier which allows an earlier start to spring cultivations.

Looking after your soil - points to remember:
- ❏ Break up subsoil to ensure good drainage.
- ❏ Practice crop rotation to prevent the build-up of pests and diseases.
- ❏ Test the pH level every third year and add lime when it falls below 6.0.
- ❏ Add compost and/or well rotted manure every year – even when growing root crops.
- ❏ Keep surface cultivations to a minimum – stop raking as soon as the desired tilth is formed.
- ❏ Do not walk on wet soil – if it dirties your shoes keep off!
- ❏ Keep the dutch hoe near to the surface. Hoe as little as possible.
- ❏ Compost crop residues and other available organic matter and return them to the soil.

RAISED BEDS

The best way to look after your soil and produce good crops is to organise the vegetable area into a series of raised beds.

Vegetables can be grown more easily by organising the growing area into raised beds and carrying out all operations from the paths. Raised beds are 1.3m (4ft) wide and once made, the beds are never walked upon; this protects the soil from compacting and gives the grower more control over plant spacings. The soil depth of the beds is increased by skimming off the soil from the paths and putting it on the beds. If the soil is very clayey or badly drained the beds can be further raised by importing soil. This enables excellent vegetables to be produced on difficult soils. Raised beds can be of any length but in practice about 3m (10ft) is a maximum, if beds are longer it becomes tiresome moving from one side to the other during some operations.

Before raised beds are constructed the soil should be worked as deeply as possible and 6kg (12lb) per sq m of fibrous organic material mixed in. This will keep the lower layers of soil open for several years and increase the volume of soil available to crop roots. On some soil annual digging may be unnecessary, if the soil has slumped during winter rains it can be forked over from the paths, otherwise light hoeing to remove weed growth followed by fertiliser application is all the preparation required.

The paths between raised beds should be as narrow as practical. Narrow paths maximise the cropping area and reduce weed growth – the paths in the photograph are 60cm (2ft) wide. Narrower paths are sometimes recommended but in practice they do not give enough working space. It is most important that **the beds are never walked upon,** untrodden soil maintains its structure and there will be no danger of forming a 'hard pan' just below the depth of cultivation.

Plants on raised beds can be grown close together as there is no need to leave access between individual rows. Closer planting reduces weed growth and produces a high yield of small vegetables. Where families are small, two small cabbages or cauliflowers are better than one large one.

Advantages of growing vegetables in raised beds:

❏ The soil does not become compacted – this gives more rooting space and increases the available water and nutrients.

❏ Annual digging is reduced and it may be possible to operate a 'no dig' system.

❏ The soil warms more quickly in spring – especially on heavy wet soil. Early sown crops are more likely to succeed.

❏ Plants can be grown closer together this
  • increases the yield.
  • suppresses weeds.
  • gives some control over the size of vegetables.

❏ Operations such as transplanting, weeding and harvesting can be carried out when the soil is too wet to be walked upon.

❏ The soil depth of the cropped area is increased.

❏ Once the beds are set up, the time needed to produce vegetables is considerably reduced.

❏ Crop rotation is easier to manage.

❏ When wooden surrounds are used there is an ideal anchor point for horticultural fleece.

❏ Weeds on paths can be controlled with chemicals. eg 'Pathclear'.

❏ The short rows make it easier to sow or plant small quantities at a time.

❏ The management of heavy soils is made much easier.

❏ The beds give a tidy, organised look to the vegetable garden.

Disadvantages of growing vegetables in raised beds:

❏ The sides of raised beds tend to dry out.

❏ Initial cost of wood to construct surrounds – if they are used.

CROP ROTATION

If the same, or a closely related crop is grown in one area year after year, soil borne pests and diseases are likely to increase. In addition some types of weed may become more troublesome. Most experts recommend a strict 3 year rotation using three groups of vegetables. In practice this is difficult to achieve as the three groups do not necessarily occupy an equal area. Brassica crops in particular are likely to take more than one third of the cropped area.

In spite of this difficulty crop rotation should be practised as far as possible and growing a vegetable from the same group in the same area 2 years running should be avoided.

GROUP 1	GROUP 2	GROUP 3
Beans	Cabbage	Carrot
Leek	Cauliflower	Parsnip
Lettuce	Brussels Sprout	Beetroot
Onion	Broccoli	Potato
Pea	Radish	Tomato
Celery	Swede	
	Turnip	

The groups should be planted in the following sequence:

	PLOT 1	PLOT 2	PLOT 3
YEAR 1	GROUP 1	GROUP 2	GROUP 3
YEAR 2	GROUP 3	GROUP 1	GROUP 2
YEAR 3	GROUP 2	GROUP 3	GROUP 1

Below left: These raised beds are 3m (10ft) long and have agricultural fencing surrounds. The wood is tanalised and will last indefinitely. The paths consist of a 5cm (2in) deep layer of quarter inch to dust-quarry waste raked level, watered and trodden firm

The autumn before Group 2 vegetables are to be grown is the best time to check for soil acidity and add lime if the pH is below 6.0. **The soil will gradually improve if well rotted organic manure is added each year.** This will not cause carrots and parsnips to fork providing the manure is well rotted. Fertiliser should be used according to the recommendations for individual crops.

Below : The same area photographed in spring and autumn. Whatever the season well organised raised beds look neat and tidy

2

VARIETIES

Varieties of gourds

When opening a seed catalogue the amateur gardener is confronted with a large selection of varieties. These differ in yield, quality, size, maturity time, disease resistance, colour and shape. The correct choice of variety is the first step to success. Knowledge of each of the following will help to make that choice:

❏ Time taken to reach maturity
❏ Continuity of supply
❏ Yield
❏ Colour
❏ Plant size
❏ Pest and disease resistance
❏ Special factors

Time taken to reach maturity

A vegetable variety that matures quickly will produce an earlier crop than one that matures slowly. Although quick maturing varieties are often referred to as 'early' varieties, they can also be used to produce a late crop. For example sowing an early variety of peas in late May would produce a crop, whereas a late variety would probably fail.

Continuity of supply

In order to achieve a regular supply of vegetables it is often necessary for the gardener to grow several varieties of the same crop. Careful selection of varieties makes it possible to harvest cabbages almost all the year round. 'Hispi' (a pointed summer cabbage) for example is the earliest variety of spring sown cabbage but its heart bursts within a week or two of maturing. 'Quickstep' (a round summer cabbage) matures later than Hispi and stands in good condition for well over a month. Hispi and Quickstep can be used to give a continuous supply of hearted cabbage from early June until late August. Other varieties must be grown in order to supply cabbage from September to May (See page 74).

Yield

With some vegetables the potential yield of a variety is important - maincrop peas for example. With other vegetables planting distances can have a greater effect on yield than variety. Examples of these are cabbages, cauliflowers and onions.

Colour

Food is often judged by its appearance – meals are seen before they are tasted! A salad with contrasting colours has more appeal than a plain green one.

Plant size

Size may be an important consideration, on a windy site a short variety of Brussels

Lettuce grown on the path between two rows of peas, ready for harvest before the path is needed for picking peas

Purple sprouting broccoli

sprouts would be better than a tall variety. It is often stated that small sized varieties are 'ideal' for small gardens, this is not true for all crops, a tall variety of peas would produce a bigger crop than a short one whilst taking no more space. The purple sprouting broccoli in the photograph however would be unsuitable for a small garden.

Pests and Disease Resistance

Some varieties are more resistant to pests and diseases than others. The advantage of a potato resistant to slugs, or a lettuce resistant to root aphids is obvious. Vegetable gardeners are advised to select varieties with inbred resistance to pests and diseases.

Special Factors

Some varieties will succeed in conditions where others fail. For example smooth seeded varieties of peas are suitable for autumn sowing whilst wrinkled seeded varieties are not. Only certain varieties of beetroot will produce a crop from an early spring sowing.

Variety Trials

The Royal Horticultural Society (RHS) conducts vegetable trials at Wisley garden in Surrey. The varieties they test are assessed and sampled by a panel of experts and the following certificates are awarded for the best:

Outstanding excellence
>First Class Certificate (FCC)

Great Merit
>Award of Merit (AM)

Good Variety
>Highly Commended (HC)

Official Government trials of vegetable varieties are carried out by the National Institute of Agricultural Botany (NIAB). These trials differ from the RHS trials in that they are done on a number of different sites throughout the country and are repeated over several years.

New Varieties

New varieties are continually being developed by plant breeders. Most of the new vegetable varieties are produced to meet the needs of the commercial grower. Some of these new varieties are suitable for the

vegetable gardener and some are not. For example a variety of carrot with a good resistance to carrot fly would be a real boon to commercial grower and amateur gardener alike. On the other hand a variety of Brussels sprout upon which all the buttons matured at the same time would be ideal for the commercial grower with a machine picker. This variety would be unsuitable for the gardener who wants to pick a few sprouts once or twice each week.

New varieties undergo a series of tests before they are allowed to be sold. In order to pass these tests a new variety has to be:

1. different from other varieties.
2. uniform throughout the crop.
3. stable from year to year.

Once official tests have been passed a new variety is added to the *National List of Vegetables for the U.K.* and the *EC Common Catalogue*. All vegetable seeds offered for sale in Europe must be in the 'National List' or the 'Common Catalogue'. Each variety has only one name and it is illegal to market a vegetable variety under more than one name.

Many old vegetable varieties, not on the list, are in danger of being lost forever. Some of these have been collected by the Institute of Horticultural Research at Wellesbourne in Warwickshire and stored in a vegetable Gene Bank. The Centre of Organic Gardening at Ryton also has a scheme to save the old varieties. There are good scientific reasons for saving old varieties, if a variety is lost genes (characteristics) will be lost as well. It is possible that the lost genes may one day be needed.

Star Variety

Each vegetable, described in chapter 11 has a 'Star' variety. In order to make this selection the author grew the whole range of vegetables from the *Kings Catalogue*. The most successful were tested for their culinary merit by a number of farmers' wives, known locally for their good cooking.

The production of F1 seeds.

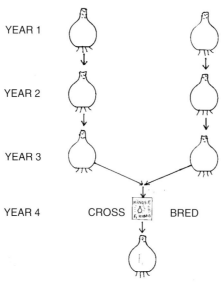

YEAR 1

YEAR 2

YEAR 3

YEAR 4   CROSS   BRED

F₁ Hybrids

An F₁ Hybrid is the first cross between two pure inbred lines. It costs more to produce hybrid seeds than it does to produce seeds of open pollinated varieties. The extra cost is passed on to the gardener, either in the form of a higher cost per packet or fewer seeds in each.

Many packets of seeds are labelled 'F₁' or 'F₁ Hybrid' or just 'Hybrid'. With some hybrid varieties the extra cost is well worth while but with others it is not. In addition to being reliable and uniform, hybrid varieties may have special characteristics, such as increased hardiness in winter cabbage, stringlessness in runner beans and blot resistance in beetroot.

There are some disadvantages with growing hybrid varieties:

The crop may mature all at once. Seeds saved from a hybrid variety will grow variable plants, some of which will be inferior.

SUCCESSION

In the vegetable garden there are times of plenty, for example in August when a bed of cauliflowers mature at the same time as a row of peas and the runner beans are in full production. As none of these vegetables remain in good condition for more than a few days a deep freezer is necessary to take care of this situation. The aim of the vegetable gardener should be to produce a year round supply of fresh vegetables – supplemented by home-frozen ones during times of shortage. The most difficult time of year is April and May when the winter crops are exhausted and the spring ones are not ready.

Methods of obtaining succession

1. The use of a greenhouse, polytunnel or cloches to grow quick maturing crops.

This is most useful in spring for producing Hispi cabbage, spinach, turnips and forcing carrots. It is also useful for late crops like endive, parsley and Chinese cabbage.

2. Making several sowings at regular intervals.

This method works fairly well for some vegetables but not all, if five rows of peas are sown at two week intervals they are extremely unlikely to produce peas over a 10 week period. The later sown rows mature more quickly and catch-up with earlier sown ones. Successional sowing of beet-root, fennel, kohlrabi, lettuce, radish, salad onions, spinach and turnips works fairly well. It is important that seeds are not sown too early; there is nothing to be gained by putting seeds into cold soil. Warming the soil by covering with clear plastic or cloches two weeks before will advance the earliest sowing by 1 week to 10 days.

Endive matures later in the year than lettuce. When blanched it is an excellent substitute

Chicory grown in summer, is forced in the dark producing a welcome winter salad

They will mature in this order:
The Sutton; Bonny Lad; Express; Jubilee Hysor; Hylon; Relon.

The actual time taken to reach maturity however will vary according to season. A single sowing of these six varieties will give a continuous supply of fresh beans for a period of 8 weeks or more. Sowing several different varieties at the same time is a useful way of obtaining a succession of cauliflowers and/or lettuce.

4. Raising plants under cover and transplanting (see also pages 27 and 28).

Almost all vegetables benefit from this method of cultivation - especially if they are grown in individual containers and moved without disturbing the root ball. The season is extended by up to 4 weeks by getting earlier crops of the following: beetroot, broad beans, calabrese, cabbage, cauliflower, courgettes, fennel, French beans, kohlrabi, lettuce, parsley, runner beans and sweetcorn. Care must be taken that some of these crops are not given a period of cold otherwise bolting will result.

5. Harvesting vegetables with long 'shelf-lives' as and when required.

Brussels sprouts, carrots, leeks, salsify, parsnips and swedes. These vegetables are best left on the plant or in the soil until required. Lifting and storing is very much a second best but may be necessary in some areas.

6. Other methods that work for individual vegetables:

Brussels sprouts: Remove the top bud of some plants in September when the sprouts are between 6 mm (1/4 in) and 12 mm (1/2in) in diameter. These plants will produce sprouts earlier than the ones with the top buds left on.

Cabbage: By use of different varieties it is possible to have cabbage ready for cutting for at least 10 months of the year – see

3. Sowing several varieties at the same time.

Some varieties take longer to mature and the order of maturity of different varieties tends to be constant regardless of soil, site or weather conditions. If the following varieties of broad beans are sown at the same time:

Bonny Lad; Relon; The Sutton; Express; Hylon; Jubilee Hysor.

chart on page 74.

Cauliflower: If transplants from a single sowing are planted out over a period of three weeks they mature over a similar period – the earliest transplants maturing first. The last transplanting must be made before the plants have stems the thickness of a pencil or buttoning will result.

Courgettes: Once fruits begin to form a continuous supply of courgettes is easy – this is achieved by regular harvesting (at least every third day) and not allowing any marrows to develop.

Lettuce: This crop, and the demand for it, is very weather dependent. Shortages and gluts are all too common. The continuous supply of hearted lettuce is more difficult than the continuous supply of leaves.

Successional sowings of leaf varieties and close planted cos types will give a continuous supply of lettuce leaves throughout the season.

Onions: The June gap in the supply of onions to the kitchen can be plugged by using Japanese types, planted in the autumn.

7. Lifting and storing.

Most root crops including potatoes, beetroot, carrots, parsnips and swedes can be stored by packing in sand (clamping). A better method is to put them (undamaged and dry) into large paper bags of the type wholesalers use for 25kg (55lb) of potatoes. These are then stored in a cold, frost free shed or garage.

BABY VEGETABLES

Although it is fun to grow very large onions, pumpkins and other vegetables, small vegetables are much more practical. It is easier to harvest the exact amount needed, which means less waste and a larger proportion eaten fresh. Smaller vegetables often give a larger total yield, although they weigh less there is more of them. It is sometimes said that small vegetables are suitable for small gardens, that may be true but small vegetables are also suitable for large gardens. Small vegetables do not always grow on small plants, a climbing French bean may be 2m (6ft) tall but it only has the same size fruit as dwarf beans.

There are three main ways of producing baby vegetables:

1. Harvesting them before they mature.
2. Growing them close together so they do not have room to become large.
3. Selecting a variety that does not grow large.

1. Harvesting them before they mature.

People have done this for years with potatoes. 'New' potatoes are small with weak undeveloped skins and if an early variety of potato is left to grow to maturity the tubers become large and the skins tough. We are lucky with potatoes as the immature ones have an excellent flavour. This does not work with all crops, taste a young lettuce and you will find that it is really bitter. Courgettes, beetroot, fennel, kohlrabi, leek and onion can be harvested before maturity.

2. Growing them close together so they do not have room to become large.

This works with some vegetables (eg. some cauliflowers) but not others (eg hearted lettuce). The Institute of Horticultural Research at Wellesbourne have researched the spacing of vegetables over several seasons. They found that cabbages spaced 14 x 14ins (35 x 35cm) gave small heads that were just the right size for the average family. The same variety spaced at 18 x 18in (45 x 45cm) gave much larger heads. They weighed the cabbages and found that close spacing produced the biggest yield.

Try growing five leeks in one hole instead of just one. The leeks will be much smaller – but you will have five of them.

Spacing is all important in mini-veg production. The chart on page 80 gives the best spacing for the production of mini-cauliflowers.

3. Selecting a variety that does not grow large (eg Tom Thumb lettuce).

Just as the growers of large onions must select varieties like Kelsae, Monkston or Mammoth, growers of mini-veg must select varieties which suit that type of production. With some species it is easy; to grow mini-tomatoes select the variety Sweet 100 and all the tomatoes will be small no matter how much space the plants have. Kings have varieties that will produce small vegetables, be careful however as some mini-vegetables grow on large plants – courgettes for example.

Small vegetables which grow on small plants are suitable for culture in pots, containers and growbags. This allows vegetable growing on patios, yards and in very small gardens.

These small cabbages grew on the old stump which was left after a large cabbage had been cut

3

SOWING
SEEDS

Seeds that are usually sown directly into the soil include parsnips, carrots, radish, beetroot, turnips, swedes, summer lettuce, spring onions, salsify, peas and spinach. Other crops can of course be sown directly into the soil but there are good reasons for raising the plants elsewhere (see page 28).

❏ Push a measuring stick (a garden cane cut to the distance required between the rows) into each end of the row and position the planting stick against them.

❏ Use the corner of a draw hoe, or an onion hoe, to draw a shallow trench. Take care to keep the hoe pressed against the planting stick. If a garden line is being used instead of a planting stick and it moves during this operation, lift it near the centre and release, the line will then fall back into its correct place.

❏ Draw a deep trench 5cm (2in) for large seeds and a shallow one 1cm (½in) for small seeds. The trench must be uniform in depth or germination will be uneven.

❏ Dribble water along the bottom of the trench. Omit this step if the soil is wet.

❏ Sprinkle seeds very thinly and evenly along the trench. This can be done by taking a pinch of seeds and releasing them a few at a time, or by holding the opened seed packet just above the trench and gen-

tly tapping it. Large seeds, like broad beans, are best individually placed.

❏ Fill the trench by very lightly raking the surplus soil back into the trench.

❏ Firm the soil above the seeds by tapping with the head of the rake.

❏ If the tilth is coarse, or the soil likely to 'cap', the seeds can be covered with a multipurpose compost instead of soil.

❏ Use the two measuring sticks to position a cane at each end of the next row and move the planting stick against them.

The soil bed in the foreground has rows of seeds which have been covered with compost instead of soil. This prevents soil capping and reduces the need for hand weeding.

Above: A measuring stick in use

Above right: Root trainer opened to show the roots of Runner beans

Below left: These two Brussels sprout plants are the same variety. The one on the right was sown March 27 and the one on the left was sown June 1

Below right: Sweetcorn and Runner beans in root trainers

TROUBLE SHOOTER – SOWING SEEDS

PROBLEM	POSSIBLE CAUSE	CORRECTION
Seedlings fail to emerge	Soil too cold	Sow later
Uneven emergence	Trench not uniform depth or trench too deep or cloddy soil	Produce a better tilth which allows more precision
Soil 'caps' (forms a crust)	Heavy rain or over worked soil or a clayey soil	Cover seeds with peat compost instead of soil or keep the crust moist by watering daily using a fine rose

SOWING GUIDE

It is most important that sowings are made at the right time. If this is done everything else follows. There is some latitude however and outside sowings must not be made in unsuitable soil conditions – *'it is better to be in tune than in time'*. The actual sowing dates obviously vary with the district and the season.

Items listed under 'greenhouse' are intended for transplanting outside.

	SOW IN GREENHOUSE (or cold frame)	SOW OUTDOORS
January	Broad beans	
	Early cauliflower	
	Onions	
February	Broad beans	
	Carrot (round varieties only)	
	Hearted lettuce	
	Hispi cabbage	
	Leek	Shallots
March	Beetroot	Onions
	Brussels sprouts	Salad onions
	Calabrese	
	Celariac	
	Celery	
	Leaf lettuce	
	Parsley	
	Peas (early)	
	Radish	
	Summer cabbage	
	Summer cauliflower	
	Tomato	
April	Courgette	Autumn cauliflower
	French beans	Beetroot
	Marrow	Broad beans
	Ridge cucumber	Calabrese
	Runner beans	Carrot
	Sweet corn	Leeks
		Lettuce
		Parsley
		Parsnips
		Peas (maincrop)
		Radish
		Spinach
		Turnips
		Winter cabbage

	SOW IN GREENHOUSE (or cold frame)	SOW OUTDOORS
May		Beetroot
		Calabrese
		Carrot
		Courgettes
		French beans
		Gourds
		Lettuce
		Marrows
		Peas (early)
		Runner beans
		Salad onions
		Sprouting broccoli
		Turnips
		Winter cabbage
		Winter cauliflower
June		Beetroot
		Chinese cabbage
		French beans
		Lettuce
		Salad onion
July		Leaf lettuce
		Spinach
August		Spring cabbage (see page 73)
		Bulb onions
		Salad onions
		Winter radish
September		Spinach
October/November		Broad beans (Aquadulce)
		Peas (smooth seeded)
		Garlic

PLANTING

By far the best method of growing vegetables is to raise plants in one area and transplant them to another. This has been practised for many years with such crops as brassicas. Plants are raised in a separate part of the garden in a 'seed bed'; they are then dug up and planted into the cropping area. Bare root transplants suffer some root damage and skilled gardeners keep the effect of this to a minimum in the following ways:

❏ Seeds are sown very thinly.
❏ The plants are watered an hour or so before lifting.
❏ The plants are not pulled up – they are lifted with a fork.
❏ Transplanting is done on a damp sunless day, if this is not possible it is done in the evening.
❏ Transplants are planted firmly and a little deeper than they were in the seed bed.
❏ After planting, the plants are given a good watering (puddled in).
❏ In sunny weather the transplants are covered with a single sheet of newspaper for a few days.

Advantages of growing by the transplanting method:

❏ Fewer seeds are needed as there are no 'thinnings' to throw away.
❏ Soil structure of the planting area is conserved as only a small area of ground has to be broken to a fine tilth.
❏ Hand weeding is reduced to a minimum and is confined to the seed bed.
❏ Weed control is easier as the cropped area is in use for a shorter period.
❏ An extra crop can be obtained. For example early potatoes could be followed by Brussels sprouts.
❏ The correct spacing is easy.

It is very much better to raise plants inside in pots or root trainers. In addition to the list above, vegetables grown under cover have the following advantages.

❏ Earlier crops can be grown.
❏ Soil borne diseases are less troublesome.
❏ Cold wet springs do not delay sowing.
❏ There is no transplanting shock as the roots are undamaged (this is particlarly important with cauliflowers).
❏ The range of crops is increased.
❏ Some pests are controlled.
❏ The range of plants that can be grown is increased.
❏ The plants are free from soil borne pests and diseases.

Raising plants in pots (or root trainers)

A cold greenhouse with an electric propagator is ideal for growing vegetable plants. If these are not available, it is possible to germinate seeds in the house and then

Seedlings on a window sill being given extra light by placing a mirror behind them.

transfer them to a coldframe.

Garden soil is unsuitable for filling pots and trays, the best material to use is a multipurpose compost. It is most important that pots and trays are filled to within a centimetre (half inch) of the top. If good plants are to be grown they must have good roots and making a bag of compost fill extra pots is false economy.

Small seeds are usually sown thinly in trays and after germination the seedlings are transferred (pricked out) to individual pots or cells. The seedlings are best pricked out before they begin to develop true leaves. Pricking out is unnecessary if the seeds are sown individually in pots or cells. The common disease of seedlings – damping off – is much less likely when seeds are sown directly into the pots. Half hardy plants (underlined in the list below) should be sown later than the others and must be protected from frost (the temperature can fall below freezing in a cold greenhouse.) Frost damage can be avoided by standing the trays on polystyrene and if frost is forecast, cover them at night with fleece and an aluminium body blanket.

Lettuce and beetroot ready for planting out

The range of plants that should be grown in this way includes:

Broad beans; <u>French beans</u>; <u>Runner beans</u>; Beetroot, Broccoli; Brussels sprouts; Cabbage; Cauliflower; Carrots (only the small round varieties); Celeriac; Celery; <u>Courgettes</u>; <u>Squashes</u>; <u>Cucumbers</u>; Endive; Fennel; <u>Gherkins</u>; Kale; Kohlrabi; Leeks; Lettuce (not midsummer varieties); Onions; Parsley; Peas (earliest crops only); <u>Peppers</u>; Radicchio; <u>Sweet Corn</u> and <u>Tomatoes</u>.

The half hardy crops are underlined.

Transplanting pot grown plants

❏ Half an hour before planting water the pots with a dilute solution of a complete plant food like Phostrogen, Miraclegro or one of the Chempak range.
❏ Rake the previously dug plot or raised bed lightly to level the soil and form a medium tilth.
❏ Position a planting board along the row (or use a garden line but a planting board is better).
❏ Use a trowel to dig a hole twice the size of the pot.
❏ Turn the pot upside-down and position the fingers over the compost to catch the plant.
❏ Release the plant by tapping the rim of the pot with the trowel.
❏ Position the plant along the planting stick with the compost level with (or if it has a long stem a little below) the soil sur face.
❏ Fill the hole around the root ball with loose soil.
❏ Firm the soil taking great care not to break the root ball.
❏ Plant the other plants in the same way, measuring the distances from plant cen tres and not from the edges of the holes.
❏ Give a good soaking with a watering can. Do not wet the whole of the soil, just the area immediately around the plants.
❏ Protect vulnerable plants with fleece or cloches.

4

FEEDING & WATERING

Fertilisers

A fertiliser is a chemical that will increase plant growth. Fertilisers work by supplying chemicals that are in short supply.

It is possible to maintain the fertility of a flower garden by recycling the waste it produces via the compost heap. This is not possible with a vegetable garden; the substances contained in the crops have been taken from the soil and must be replaced. If this is not done the soil will gradually become impoverished and yields will decline. Fertility is maintained by adding manures or fertilisers or some of each.

Feeding Plants

Plants need fifteen different elements in order to grow and remain healthy. Hydrogen and oxygen are obtained from water and carbon from the air. The other twelve are taken from the soil. Six elements are needed in very small amounts; these are called 'trace elements' or 'micro nutrients'. Six others are used in larger quantities, they are:

- ❏ Sulphur
- ❏ Magnesium
- ❏ Calcium
- ❏ Nitrogen
- ❏ Phosphorus
- ❏ Potassium

Various Chempak fertilisers

Sulphur. Almost all soils have ample reserves of sulphur and this element is most unlikely to be deficient. Sulphur is present in many fertilisers and it also falls in acid rain.

Magnesium. Plants sometimes become deficient in magnesium; the symptoms of this are pale, yellow areas between the leaf veins (chlorosis). *Epsom salts sprayed onto the leaves will correct this in the short term and an application of magnesium limestone to the soil will correct it in the longer term. * 20g per l (3oz per gal)

Calcium. The amount of calcium present in a soil affects its pH (acidity). Calcium is present in lime which is used to correct a low pH. If the pH is around 6.5 the level of calcium will be correct. Too much or too little lime will reduce the availability of some trace elements. The amount of lime to add is given on page 9.

Calcium deficiency causes defects in plants, the young leaves curl upwards forming cups, the edge of lettuce leaves turn brown (tip burn) and the insides of Brussels sprouts are brown.

Nitrogen. Nitrogen is the key to vigorous, healthy growth. Plants need a lot of nitrogen as it forms 3% of their tissues. Nitrogen fertiliser is soluble and easily washed out of the soil. Plants absorb nitrogen in the form of nitrates; gardeners therefore talk of nitrate rather than nitrogen.

Phosphorus. Phosphorus is responsible for good rooting systems and it is necessary to ensure adequate supplies are available. It is absorbed by plants in the form of phosphate.

Potassium. Potassium is used during flower and fruit formation. The common name is potash.

If a plant is short of a chemical it cannot grow well, adding this chemical will improve growth. Chemicals that improve plant growth are called fertilisers. Nitrate, phosphate and potash are the three substances that are most likely to be in short supply, they are therefore applied as fertilisers. Some packets of fertiliser use the chemists' shorthand, this is:

N for nitrate,
P for phosphate
K for potash.

The proportions of each plant food is given in the order N, P, K. A fertiliser packet which has 10 : 5 : 20 will contain 10% nitrate, 5% phosphate and 20% potash. As this fertiliser contains all three plant foods it is called a complete fertiliser.

It is possible to give too much fertiliser and this is as bad as giving too little. Too much nitrogen for example causes plants to grow rank and soft stemmed; it also delays the ripening of fruit.

THE EFFECTS OF NITRATE, PHOSPHATE AND POTASH ON PLANTS

Fertiliser	Part most affected	Signs of shortage	Effect of adding too much
Nitrate	Leaves	Yellow colour leaves	Rank, spindly growth delayed maturity
Phosphate	Roots	Poor growth, blue colour leaves	Effects not easily seen
Potash	Flowers and fruit	Leaf margins die	New growth small and tinged with blue

Trace elements (micro nutrients)

These are: zinc, iron, maganese, boron, copper and molybdenum. Shortages can cause various problems including yellow mottling of the leaves, pale leaves with dark green veins, dead buds, beetroots with black crowns and cauliflowers with strap-like leaves. These symptoms can be treated by spraying with a solution of trace elements (obtained from garden centres).

Organic or Inorganic fertilisers?

Organic fertilisers consist of material that was once alive, blood, bone and hooves for example. Soil bacteria break organic ferti-liser down into simple chemicals. It is these simple chemicals that are absorbed by plant roots.

Inorganic fertilisers consist of the sim-ple chemicals – the same chemicals are absorbed regardless of the type of fertiliser used.

Some organic fertilisers (eg bonemeal) release plant foods over a period of time, this gives a continuous supply. Others (eg dried blood) release plant foods very quickly. Slow release chemical fertilisers are available; these are fine in hanging bas-kets but too expensive for general use in the vegetable garden.

Bulky organic fertilisers improve the structure of the soil whilst inorganic ferti-lisers do not.

Organic gardeners claim to feed the soil and not the plants and this claim contains a lot of truth.

How much fertiliser to apply.

It is better to err on the side of too little than to give too much. Too little fertiliser will reduce the size of the crop but too much is harmful and can even kill the crop. How much depends upon the crop as different plants have different requirements. The best way is to apply phosphate and potash to the whole garden once a year and add the nitrate as needed. *The needs of individual vegetables is given in Chapter 11, pages 66 – 120.*

If large quantities (5 kg sq metre / 10 lb sq yd) of farm yard manure, stable manure or compost are applied each year there will probably be sufficient phosphate and pot-ash in the soil. Where manures are in short supply:

1. Spread 35g per sq m (1oz sq yd) of sul-phate of potash over the soil before autumn or early spring digging.
2. Apply 70g per sq m (2oz sq yd) of super-phosphate. Research has shown that this is more effective when placed in bands 5 cm

(2in) to the side and 7cm (3in) below the row of seeds or plants.

If a compound fertiliser is being used to supply nitrate then there is no need to add phosphate and potash separately. This is more expensive than the methods sug-gested above and excessive amounts of phosphate and potash may be added in order to get the correct amount of nitrate.

In Chapter 11 all the rates of fertiliser application are given for 10% nitrate ferti-liser. Use the table below to find how much fertiliser you need. Metric example: If you are using Nitrate of soda (N = 15%) and Chapter 11 suggests 60g per sq m (10% N). Read the figure in the 15% column which is level with 60g in the 10% column the answer is 45g.

Imperial example: If you are using Ni-trate of soda (N = 15%) and Chapter 11 suggests 2oz. per sq yd (10% N). Read the figure in the 15% column which is level with 2oz in the 10% column the answer is 1oz.

Beans and peas have nodules on their roots. These are full of bacteria which make nitrogen fertiliser from the air in the soil

Table to convert fertiliser applications from one strength of fertiliser to another

5% nitrate fertiliser per sq m [per sq yd]		10% nitrate fertiliser per sq m [per sq yd]		15% nitrate fertiliser per sq m [per sq yd]		20% nitrate fertiliser per sq m [per sq yd]	
grams	ounces	grams	ounces	grams	ounces	grams	ounces
50	2	25	1	18	½	12	½
100	4	50	2	37	1½	25	1
120	4½	60	2	45	1½	30	1
140	5	70	2½	52	2	35	1
160	6	80	3	60	2	40	1½
200	8	100	4	75	3	50	2
240	9	120	4½	90	3½	60	2
300	11	150	5½	122	4	75	3
340	12	170	6	127	5	85	3

The percentages of nitrate present in different fertilisers

Fertiliser	Percentage of nitrate
Sulphate of ammonia	21
Nitrochalk	21
Nitrate of soda	15
Calcium nitrate	15
Hoof and horn	14
Dried blood	14 (some samples may be a little less)
Fish meal	9

When to apply fertilisers.

Phosphate and potash are not washed out of the soil by rain and these may be applied at any time.

Nitrates are easily washed out of the soil; they may also harm seedlings and severely depress germination levels. Damage is avoided by applying half the nitrate to the seed or plant bed and the other half 6 weeks later.

How to apply fertilisers

Fertilisers are available in three forms, liquid, powder and granules. The liquids are diluted and watered on with a rose can. Some powders are formulated to be applied in a similar way. Other powders are less soluble and are spread over the surface and either watered or raked in. Granules are spread on the surface; these may or may not be raked into the surface.

Applying a fertiliser to the soil surface around growing plants, is known as 'top dressing'.

The advantages and disadvantages of liquids, powders and granules are shown in the table below.

	Advantages	Disadvantages
Liquids & soluble powders	The fertiliser quickly reaches the roots. When watered over the plants, some may be absorbed by the leaves – foliar feeding. The better ones contain trace elements.	Expensive.
Powders	Cheap.	Can be difficult to apply, especially in wind.
Granules	Very easy to apply evenly. Plant foods are released more slowly. No water required for application.	None.

Watering

Plants need water for three reasons:

1. To transport chemicals from the soil to leaves.
2. As a raw material to make sugars.
3. To remain turgid (stiff). [Plant cells are blown up with water in a similar way to car tyres being blown up with air.]

A plant acts like a wick, continually taking water from the soil and evaporating it into the air. The speed at which water flows through a plant varies, wind and sun increase the rate, whilst cold, damp and dark reduces it. The soil is a reservoir and the amount it holds varies according to soil depth and type. A light sand will hold only 30 litres for each square metre of soil (6 gal sq yd) whilst a clay soil holds up to 120 litres for each square metre of soil (25 gal sq yd). Only about half of this water is available to the plants, the rest of it sticks to the soil so hard that the plant cannot draw it off. Manuring soil each year with 5kg per sq m (10lb sq yd) increases the water holding capacity by 40%. For manure to have its full effect it must be mixed with the soil as deeply as possible, dumping manure in the bottom of a trench (common practice for runner beans) does little to improve the water holding capacity.

When to water.

Knowing when to water is one of the skills of gardening. When to water varies with the soil, the crop and the weather. Wilting plants obviously need water but they should have been watered before they wilted. The best time to inspect plants is in mid-afternoon during hot sun, if there is no sign of wilting, watering is probably unnecessary. The time to water depends upon the type of crop and the state of its growth. Information about watering particular crops is given in Chapter 11 pages 66 to 120.

Some watering is more useful than others and there are times when it is vital. If

A plant pot sunk alongside a courgette plant to take water directly to the roots

water is in short supply it should be saved for the following uses:

- ❑ In the bottom of a seed drill before sowing the seeds.
- ❑ Applied to plants before they are lifted (or removed from their pots) for trans planting.
- ❑ Transplants soon after planting.
- ❑ Peas and beans coming into flower.
- ❑ Potatoes which are just forming new tubers.
- ❑ Plants that are suffering root damage (e g clubroot or cabbage root fly).
- ❑ Plants that are wilting.

How much water.

Watering plants is rather like putting petrol into a car. We wait until the level in the tank is low and then we either add a few litres or fill it up. Unlike petrol, a small amount of water is no use and may even be harmful; the aim of watering is to top-up low soil water reserves. Too much water is wasteful, it washes nitrates from the soil and can spoil the flavour of some vegetables. Too little water is a waste of time as it will be lost by evaporation before the roots have a

Above left: Watering leeks which have just been planted

Above right: A length of old down spout guides the hosepipe around the corner of the plant bed protecting the plants from damage

chance to absorb it. The minimum amount of water to give is 11 litres on each square metre (2 gallons on a square yard). This may seem a lot of water but it is only equivalent to a centimetre (half an inch) of rain. It is enough to increase the reserves and it will be at least a week before watering is needed again.

It is easy to apply too much water when using a sprinkler on the mains. The amount given can be checked by placing two or three vertical sided containers in various positions under the spray. When the water in these is 1cm (½in) deep the spray should be turned off. There are times when a small amount of water is useful; 150ml (¼pint) poured at the base of a small transplant each day will help to get it established.

Too little

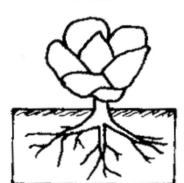

Water soon lost
through evaporation

Too much

Water drains through the soil
taking nitrates with it

Just right

Root zone wetted, no drainage

5
TOOLS

There is a very wide range of tools available including over thirty different kinds of hoe. Fortunately only the seven tools listed below are essential for vegetable production.

Spade; Fork; Rake; Dutch hoe; Draw hoe; Trowel; Watering can.

If raised beds are used then the draw hoe can be replaced with an onion hoe. A wheel-

An onion hoe in use

barrow is also a very useful aid.

All the tools are steel with wooden or plastic handles. As steel soon rusts it is necessary to oil bare parts before putting them away for any length of time. This is particularly true of the spade, a rusty spade is impossible to work with and badly organised gardeners should invest in a stainless steel one.

The British spade is seldom used in other parts of the world as it can cause back problems. The American spade is a superior tool as it has a pointed blade and long handle. It is both easy to use and kind to the back.

The Rotavator

A rotavator is a useful aid for a large neglected plot. It is easy to use providing the correct procedure is followed. When the handles are held down the rotors dig in, when the handles are raised the machine moves forward. The skill is to move the handles up and down slightly to make the machine dig at a constant depth as it travels forward. This makes for very light and easy work. However if the machine is driven into a corner it has to be manhandled out which is no mean feat. Some machines have a reverse gear which prevents this problem, when a machine is being hired I would recommend one of these.

If a garden is rotavated several times it is possible that a hard pan is created just below the depth of cultivation. This will have a detrimental effect on soil drainage and rooting systems. Clay soils are very vulnerable to pan formation and gardeners on this type of soil are advised to take extra care.

Small, light machines are sometimes advertised as being 'ideal for inter-row cultivations'. However inter-row cultivations should be kept to a minimum as many vegetables have roots near to the surface that would be damaged by this action.

Above right: the American spade is pointed and has a larger handle than the British spade

Right: The Dutch hoe is excellent for controlling seedling weeds. Only disturb the top cm (½in) of soil

Far right: An onion hoe

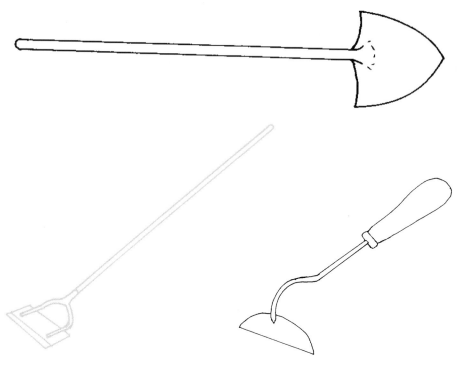

A rotavator is an expensive machine to buy but quite reasonable to hire

6

THE COMPOST HEAP

Courgette growing in a hot bed

Every garden produces organic waste such as weeds and the inedible parts of plants. If this waste is kept in a neat and organised way it will decay fairly quickly and the resulting material can be returned to the soil as compost either by digging in or using as a mulch. Good compost is a friable material which improves soil structure and provides plant foods. The conversion of waste into compost is carried out by bacteria and fungi that live in, and feed upon the waste. There are two different groups of these creatures; both groups produce compost but in a different way.

Group one (aerobic) need air, water and nitrates in addition to the waste material which is their food.
Group two (anaerobic) survive without air.

Compost can be made by two different methods, one with air and the other without air.

Method 1.

As air is necessary the heap must not be too high or too wide otherwise air will not reach the centre. 1.2 metres (4ft) wide and 1.2 m (4ft) high is about right and the length is not important. The heap is best kept in shape by open sides such as wooden slats.

The heap is built up in layers of various materials, it is better to have fairly thin layers (especially with grass clippings). Wherever possible two layers of soft mate-

rial should be kept apart by a layer of coarse material. A handful of topsoil scattered over will provide additional bacteria. A little sulphate of ammonia and a little lime sprinkled over each layer will speed the process and prevent acids from forming. (Organic gardeners can use dried blood and lime.) Any dry material is wetted and when the heap is 1.2 metres (4ft) high a piece of old carpet or similar placed on top will help to retain heat. The heap is left to heat up and the centre should reach 82°C (180°F) in ten days or so. Two weeks later the heap will need turning, the outside material being placed in the centre as far as possible. The heap is then left until ready or until required.

Method 2

A large sealed plastic bag or purpose made bin is ideal for this method. No fertiliser or lime is needed but a handful of soil sprinkled over each layer is very helpful as it increases the numbers of bacteria. This method takes longer than the first one described but it is easier and the resulting compost will probably contain more plant nutrients.

Making compost is a slow process and takes more time than the bin manufacturers' advertisements indicate. The compost is ready for use when the contents cannot be recognised and the material is brown and friable.

Materials for composting:

❏ Prunings (shredded if woody).
❏ Weeds (roots of perennial weeds are best killed by drying before being composted).
❏ Unwanted plants.
❏ Vegetable trimmings.
❏ Pea and bean straw.
❏ Grass clippings.
❏ Straw (care – has it been sprayed with herbicide?)
❏ Kitchen waste.
❏ Rabbit litter and droppings.
❏ Chicken and other manure.
❏ Seaweed.

Materials that should not be composted:

❏ Brussels sprout and cabbage stalks (unless shredded).
❏ Weeds that have been treated with herbicide.
❏ Cat litter.
❏ Brassica roots with clubroot.
❏ Clippings from lawns that have been recently treated with weed killers.

Autumn leaves are best composted on their own; chicken wire formed into a metre cube makes an ideal container. At least one year is needed for breakdown to occur, the resulting material (leafmould) is well worth the wait.

Hotbeds

In spring the soil temperature is all important – it is the increase in soil temperature, not air temperature, which starts plants into growth. If you can get some fresh stable

Fresh strawy stable manure is ideal for a hotbed but must be composted before digging into the soil

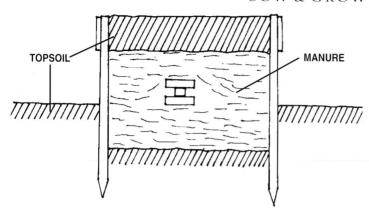

TOPSOIL

MANURE

Section through a hotbed

(or farmyard) manure, you can warm up a small area of soil with a hotbed.

How to make a hotbed

1. Drive four stakes into the soil, one in each corner.
2. Dig out the top soil and pile it up along side.
3. Spread two barrow loads of fresh, strawy stable manure over the bottom.

4. Place three old house bricks in a pile in the centre, the middle brick at right an gles to the other two. (This helps to keep some air in the centre of the hotbed).
5. Add two or three more barrow loads of manure on top to bring the height to over 120cm (4ft).
6. Leave the bed for 5 days to warm up and sink.
7. Nail four boards (plywood offcuts) each 30 cm (1 ft) wide to the posts with the tops of the boards level with the top of the bed.
8. Pile some of the topsoil on to the top of the manure.
9. Three days later when the bed has sunk shovel the rest of the soil on and level off.
10. Plant up 2 days later.

If the hotbed is in a polytunnel ·or green-house it will not require any cover, if it is outside cover the plants with cloches or a cold frame.

An ideal compost bin, the material in one section is maturing while the other section is being filled.

7

WEEDS

Weed control is an essential part of vegetable gardening. It is very easy as long as the gardener remains in control and never allows weeds to take over.

Types of Weeds

There are two types of weeds, annuals and perennials, all weeds grow from seeds and some of the perennials also propagate themselves from roots and stems. The types that are present in a garden depend largely upon the garden's history. A neglected garden will probably have the types of weeds that are most difficult to control.

Annual Weeds

This group of weeds grow only from seeds; the plants germinate, flower and seed in one growing season. Some are very short lived and have several generations in a year. Every garden contains many thousands of weed seeds, some of which will 'keep' for 20 years or more and only germinate when conditions become suitable. Whenever the soil is disturbed the conditions for some of the seeds present will change for the better and they will germinate.

This group includes: chickweed, fathen, groundsel, annual nettle, meadow grass, spurge, mayweed, knotgrass, shepherd's purse and many others.

Most annual weeds have the potential to produce hundreds and possibly thousands of seeds, it follows that they should be re-moved before these seeds are produced.

Perennial weeds

Perennial weeds are the most difficult to control as they survive the winter and re-grow from underground parts. Unlike annuals, if they are chopped off with a hoe they regrow, they also produce flowers and seeds. A potato can become a difficult perennial weed, especially if a shoot appears in a row of spring onions! Some perennial weeds spread on the surface of the soil; buttercup for example sends runners in all directions.

This group includes:
nettle, couchgrass, ground elder and bind-weed (convolvulus).

Weed Control

Why control weeds?

Weeds give a garden an uncared for and untidy appearance. The main reason for weed control is to enable good crops to be grown. Weeds are opportunist plants and have the same requirements as the crops we are trying to grow. They need water, nutrients, space and light and any taken by the weeds are not available for the crop. Crop losses due to weeds vary from negligible to total – depending upon the comparative size of weeds and crop.

These weeds are unlikely to affect the crop of sweetcorn. They can be pulled up along with the crop plants after harvest

Some disease viruses spend the winter in weeds. For example chickweed, shepherd's purse and groundsel carry viruses that cause yellows and mosaic type diseases in lettuces, courgettes and cauliflowers. In the spring the viruses are carried from weed to plant by aphids. A blitz on weeds in late autumn will help to control these and other diseases.

Not all weeds are bad, ground beetles spend the winter in the grasses that grow under hedges. In spring the beetles move into the garden and feed on aphids many of which are consumed before they can establish colonies.

Methods of Control

The most important part of weed control is timing. Weeds must be controlled before they produce seeds, if this is done, weed control becomes easier year by year. Weeds must also be controlled before they begin to compete with crop plants, when weeds and crop germinate together, competition begins some 3 weeks after emergence. Finally all weeds should be removed in late autumn.

Physical

Physical methods include digging, hoeing and hand pulling. When digging, it is good practice to skim the weeds off the surface with a spade and bury them in the trench where they act as green manure. Roots and rhizomes (underground stems) of perennials are removed during digging; these can be composted, providing the compost heap gets hot enough to kill them.

There are over twenty different styles of hoe on the market, the traditional vegetable gardener requires two – the dutch hoe and the draw hoe – and the raised bed gardener needs only one, the onion hoe. In the interests of the soil structure, all hoeing should be kept to the absolute minimum required to control weeds. In the interests of the plants, the depth of hoeing should also be kept to the absolute minimum. Many vegetables have fine roots near to the surface and hoeing will obviously destroy these. The belief that regular hoeing leaves a dry surface mulch that conserves moisture has not been proven by scientific experiment and is probably an old wives' tale.

Another physical method, which is becoming increasingly popular is the exclusion of light. A layer of opaque black plastic held over the soil surface weakens established perennials and kills germinating weed seedlings. It is not usually practical to leave plastic on the soil long enough to kill established perennials, one way around this problem is to cut slits in the plastic and plant brassicas etcetera through the slits.

A third physical method, which reduces the hand weeding of seedlings, is to use the spade to make a wedge shape slit in the soil the full length of the row. The slit is then filled with a multi-purpose compost in which the seeds are sown. This method is excellent for slow germinating crops like parsnips and enables straight carrots to be grown in stony or clayey soils. A further advantage of this method is that it eliminates the problem of soil capping.

Chemical

There are many herbicides on the market, most of which have no place in the vegetable garden. There is however one chemical which is invaluable when cleaning up a neglected weedy garden and that is **glyphosate** (this is sold under the names Tough Weed and Roundup). It is a systemic herbicide which means that the spray enters one part of the plant (in this case the leaves) and moves through the stems to other parts.

Glyphosate is the most effective in spring **when the weeds are growing well and there is lots of foliage.** The whole area is sprayed with glyphosate applied with a garden sprayer or a fine rose watering can. A spray is more effective, the aim is to dampen, rather than wet the leaves. The foliage must be dry before spraying starts and there must be at least six rain-free hours afterwards. It is about 3 weeks before any response to spraying is seen, after that time the weeds turn brown and die. The advantage of this chemical is that the underground parts of perennial weeds are killed and will not regrow. Glyphosate works extremely well on couch grass but less well on convolvulus (bindweed) and ground elder which may produce some regrowth and require further treatment.

Glyphosate is also available as a wipe on gel; individual leaves of troublesome weeds can be brushed without the fear of harming nearby crops. Glyphosate is inactivated within minutes of reaching the soil and it is quite safe to sow and plant soon after spraying.

Weed Control in the Vegetable Garden

1. The neglected garden.

A neglected garden probably contains a high proportion of perennial weeds as well as many thousands of weed seeds in each square metre of soil. Three methods of dealing with this situation are available to the gardener.

The first is the most difficult. The garden is dug, preferably with a fork, the annual weeds are buried and the underground parts of perennial weeds removed.

The second method is to cover the area with opaque black plastic and leave it for a year. The weeds will die through lack of light. Some cropping maybe possible by planting strong plants through slits cut in the plastic.

The area can then be dug the following spring and cropped with potatoes, brassicas, beans and other plants. All seedling weeds should be controlled while still in the seedling stage by hoeing. Crops that are grown from small seeds such as carrots, turnips and spring onions should not be grown until the following year. Hand weeding of these crops is reduced if the drills are covered with a multi-purpose compost instead of soil.

The third method is to wait until the weeds are actively growing and then spray the whole area with glyphosate. Wait at least 2 weeks for the herbicide to reach all

This chickweed is taking all the available light and the row of carrots and the row of spring onions underneath are both lost.

CHEMICALS CAN BE DANGEROUS!

When using chemicals in the garden the manufacturers' instructions must be followed to the letter. The recommended strength of solutions must not be exceeded and all safety instructions heeded.

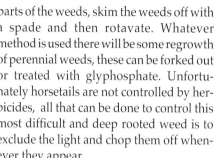

A mixture of seedling weeds. The annuals should not be allowed to seed. The perennials (eg dock) should not be chopped off with a Dutch hoe but have their underground parts removed.

parts of the weeds, skim the weeds off with a spade and then rotavate. Whatever method is used there will be some regrowth of perennial weeds, these can be forked out or treated with glyphosate. Unfortunately horsetails are not controlled by herbicides, all that can be done to control this most difficult and deep rooted weed is to exclude the light and chop them off whenever they appear.

2. The established garden.

Crop rotation is a useful aid to weed control as no plot has a regular pattern of operations. This prevents the weeds that would benefit from a regular cycle from becoming too well established.

Wherever possible plants should be raised in pots or root trainers and transplanted. This assists weed control in a number of ways:

• Crop and weeds are not germinating together; this eliminates the need for hand weeding.
• The crop is in the ground for a shorter time; there is less time for the weeds to grow.
• The crop has a head start, grows quickly and soon overshadows germinating weeds, robbing them of the light they need.

Crops that do not transplant easily, for example turnips, carrots and parsnips should be carefully hand weeded within 3 weeks of germinating as, after this time, weed competition begins to affect yields (or prevent weed growth by covering the seeds with compost instead of soil).

Some weed seeds will germinate at lower temperatures than most crop plants and the weeds appear before the crop. To combat this do not sow until the soil is warm enough for rapid germination.

Use a dutch hoe between the rows or if gardening with raised beds use an onion hoe between the plants. Weed seedlings that have been chopped off with the hoe are best left on the soil to provide food for the worms.

8
P E S T S

Vegetables provide food for creatures other than the gardener. Part of the skill in gardening is to have the lion's share of produce. Not every creature which eats plants is a problem, it is just the few which reduce yields or spoil produce. Creatures that cause significant amounts of damage are called pests and these come in all shapes and sizes from rabbits and pigeons to slugs and aphids. The gardener should never attempt to kill everything that moves by laying poisons and spraying pesticides. The vast majority of garden creatures are harmless and some are beneficial; these include insects which pollinate, insects that prey on pest species, spiders (not the red ones!), earthworms that improve the soil and birds that eat slugs – a complete list would fill pages!

Integrated Pest Management

Integrated pest management is the modern method of controlling pests. The gardener understands the creatures he/she is attempting to control and uses a variety of different methods to protect the crops whilst doing minimum damage to the other wildlife in the garden. This is much better (and cheaper and more effective) than relying upon chemical sprays alone. There are powerful reasons why too many chemicals should not be used and organic gardeners get on very well without them. Integrated pest management protects

Brussels sprout leaves distorted by colonies of cabbage aphids

Aubergine leaves. The one on the left is showing typical red spider damage

crops and wildlife.

Methods of Control

The methods of controlling pests in the vegetable garden include:

Baits; Barriers; Biological control; Chemical sprays; Crop rotation; Cropping out of season; Encouraging predators; Garden hygiene; Hand removal; Harvesting and storing; Inter cropping; Resistant varieties; Scaring; Trapping.

Note: Several of the new chemical sprays will kill the pest without killing bees and other creatures. Select these chemicals rather than general insecticides.

PESTS AND HOW TO CONTROL THEM

Pests that are most often present in the vegetable garden:

Aphids

Aphids are small insects which breed at an alarming rate. They feed by sucking plant juices; this makes the plants sticky and deprives them of the materials needed for growth. In addition when aphids move from plant to plant they spread virus diseases in a similar way in which the mosquito spreads malaria.

There are many different types of aphids and the aphid that affects roses is different from the one that affects beans. A few types of aphids feed on a variety of plants and it is one of these – the peach-potato aphid – which prevents gardeners from saving their own seed potatoes from year to year. The two aphids which are most troublesome in the vegetable garden are the black bean aphid and the cabbage aphid. The bean aphid is black and forms colonies on the tops of broad beans, these soon move down the plant to affect the buds, a badly affected plant fails to produce a crop. Runner beans may also be affected. The cabbage aphid is dark grey and forms dense colonies on the underside of brassica leaves, distorting the foliage. This aphid sometimes moves into Brussels sprout buttons, completely spoiling them. Aphids have many natural predators including birds, ground beetles, hoverfly larvae, lacewing larvae and the common ladybird.

Control

All aphids can be readily controlled with systemic insecticides; this type of insecticide moves into the plant and poisons the aphids' food. Systemic insecticides tend to move upwards; it is therefore better to spray the lower leaves even though the aphids are near to the tops of the plants. Many gardeners prefer not to use these on food crops and resort to cultural methods. Broad beans can be protected by removing the tops of the plants before the aphids arrive, the broken off stem is not a very attractive site for incoming aphids and they fly away to seek a more favourable landing place. Broad beans, grown from greenhouse raised plants will be fruiting before the aphids arrive, the crop is then unaffected. Cabbage aphids can be controlled by keeping a sharp lookout for distorted leaves and then crushing the patches of aphids between finger and thumb. The use of fleece as a barrier to prevent flying aphids from landing is also an effective method of protecting brassicas. This latter method must not to be used on crops that require pollination as the pollinating insects will also be excluded.

Birds

The pigeon has a large appetite and will quickly destroy a row of brassica transplants; model hawks and scarecrows are effective for a very limited period. The only safe way is to cover the plants with fleece.

House sparrows have a liking for germinating peas, lettuce seedlings and transplants. The only effective way of preventing damage is to cover with cloches, nets, black cotton or fleece. The covers must be positioned soon after transplanting as small plants disappear in a single visit. This problem is worse in early spring; protection is seldom necessary later in the year when other types of bird food are available.

Caterpillars

These are the larvae of butterflies and moths that feed on all parts of plants, they are most troublesome on brassica crops where they eat only the leaves. The plants are damaged by leaf loss and by frass (droppings) which is unsightly especially on the curds of cauliflowers. Large white butterfly caterpillars are usually present in groups on individual plants which they soon reduce to a skeleton, other plants nearby remaining undamaged. Small white butterfly caterpillars (the pale green ones) are found in ones or twos on most plants often feeding in the growing point. Cabbage moth caterpillars are darker in colour and feed at night.

Control

Hand picking is a good method of control but to be effective it must be done whilst the caterpillars are small. Large caterpillars have already done the damage! Crushing the eggs is an even better way of controlling; large white butterflies eggs are easy to find as they are laid in groups under the

leaves. The eggs of the small white butterfly are laid singly and are much more difficult to find. Insecticide sprays, especially those which contain pyrethrum, are effective. Another spray that is available contains a bacterial disease; this is effective but takes longer to act.

Bird damage to transplants

Cabbage caterpillars

Cabbage root fly

This insect looks like a rather leggy house-fly. It lays its eggs near to young brassica plants, the eggs hatch and the larvae feed on the plants' roots. Root loss causes young plants to become stunted and they wilt in sunshine during dry weather. The plants either die or produce a very inferior crop. All brassicas are subject to this damage but cauliflowers are most at risk. Bare root transplants are particularly vulnerable and must be protected as a matter of course.

Control

There are three control methods all of which are successful:

1. A large pinch of insecticide (wear gloves!) at the base of transplants within 3 days of planting. For radish a little insecticide in with the seeds gives some control.

2. Cutting a 15cm (6in) disc of carpet foam and making a slit to the centre. This fits around the stem and either prevents the fly from laying or provides shelter for beetles which then eat the eggs. Purchased 'brassica collars' may give a third layer of protection as many are impregnated with insecticide.

This young brassica has cabbage root fly maggots feeding on its roots

3. Covering the plants with fleece – held in position by stapling onto wooden laths. If extra fleece is wound around on to the laths it can be released as the plants grow. The last method is by far the best as it also protects from rabbits and birds and, later in the season, from caterpillars as well.

Carrot fly

This small iridescent insect appears in May and is attracted by the smell of carrot. It flies rather low and lays eggs near the favoured host – carrots. The eggs hatch in about a week and the larvae feed on the fine external roots; this feeding causes changes in the carrots' leaves and they turn from green to a pale reddish colour. If the infestation is heavy the plants wilt and die. The second generation appear in July and August, the larva burrow into the roots and spoil the carrots by making rust coloured tunnels. The damage increases with time and any crops that are showing signs of infection should be lifted, any undamaged carrots can be stored. The advice, given later in this book, to store carrots in the ground until required does not apply when carrot root fly is present. Carrot fly larvae will also feed on the roots of parsnips, parsley and celery.

Control

1. Various insecticides are effective against carrot fly; two or three applications may have to be made as persistent chemicals are not available to gardeners. The insecticide is applied to the soil, either in the seed bed or alongside the row soon after germination.

2. Carrots sown in June are less likely to be damaged than those sown in May and July.

3. Sowing seeds thinly to avoid thinning out the plants later (when the smell of disturbed carrots attracts the flies).

4. Harvesting just before dark and treading the soil along both sides of the rows afterwards, is said to make laying sites less favourable, the author is not aware of any controlled trials which support or refute this.

5. A very effective method of controlling carrot root fly is to have a vertical barrier of fleece about a metre (yard) high all around the carrot bed. The top can be left open as the fly stays near to the ground when searching for laying sites. Clear plastic can be used instead of fleece but it is more likely to suffer wind damage.

6. Carrots (and parsnips and parsley) which show signs of infection should be lifted before November. The reason for this is two fold, first damage increases during the winter and secondly, the longer the roots are in the ground the more larvae will form pupae. These pupae survive in the soil and emerge to infect next year's crop.

Cutworms

The larvae of several species of moth are collectively called 'cutworms'. They arise from eggs which are usually laid on weeds, after feeding on leaves for a week or so they drop onto the soil and feed on plant stems at ground level. This either cuts the plant off cleanly or leaves it to blow over in the wind. Any crop may be attacked but damage is usually worst on brassicas and lettuce. The larvae are plump, 5cm (2in) long and coloured brown, yellow or green. They feed at night and can easily be found with the aid of a torch.

Control

1. A weed free garden is less likely to have cut worm problems than a weedy one. Weed control is therefore the first line of defence. Autumn digging will help to expose some larvae to birds and other predators.

2. If a plant is found which has been severed at ground level, a search in nearby soil will often reveal the culprit which can then be destroyed.

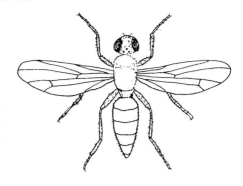

Carrot fly

3. On very susceptible gardens, a cover of fleece will prevent the moths from laying their eggs.

4. If all else fails a sprinkling of insecticide around the base of transplants will help to protect them.

Eelworms (nematodes)

Eelworms themselves are too small to be seen but the bodies of females swollen with eggs are just visible on the roots of infected potatoes. They are unsegmented worms that feed on plant stems, roots and root hairs. The dead bodies of females are called cysts and these contain eggs that will survive in the soil for up to ten years. Any susceptible plant growing nearby will cause the eggs to hatch. One species (stem nematode) causes stunted seedlings and thick necks in onions and leeks. The most common one is the potato cyst nematode which feeds on potato and tomato roots. The infected plants are stunted and grow slowly producing a very small crop of inferior tubers or fruit.

Control

Crop rotation is the only method of control available to gardeners. Tomatoes can be grown in growbags, straw bales or containers instead of the garden plot. Potatoes should be given a 6 year rotation to avoid eelworms. This is done by growing potatoes in one half of the Group 3 plot during one cycle and in the other half during the following cycle. Some potato varieties are

Woodmouse

more resistant to eelworms than others, Maris Piper for example. Resistant varieties are only an aid to control and must be subject to crop rotation.

Flea beetles

These tiny beetles (3mm long - about a $\frac{1}{10}$in) can be seen on sunny days in April and May feeding on the seed leaves of brassicas. They jump when disturbed – hence the name. After overwintering in weeds and hedge bottoms the adults lay eggs near to brassicas. The larvae feed on the roots and leaves and do little damage. The second generation of adults feed on seed leaves of germinating brassicas (turnips, swedes, cauliflowers etc), the first sign of damage is tiny holes in the seed leaves. The seedlings are soon destroyed and the whole crop may be lost, damage is particularly severe in dry weather when emergence is often slow.

Control

1. Early sowings (March) or late sowings (June) are not effected and this gives a control method for some crops such as Brussels sprouts and swedes.

2. A seed bed covered with fleece has almost 100% protection.

3. Some insecticide powders dusted on the emerging crop give good control.

Leatherjackets

These tough dark coloured grubs are the larvae of the cranefly (daddy longlegs). The damage they cause and the methods of control are the same as for cutworms (above) except that a covering of fleece will not work as the eggs are laid during the previous autumn.

Mice

Germinating peas and broad beans are often dug up, the seed is eaten and the shoot discarded. This damage is unlikely to be caused by house mice – wood mice are probably responsible.

Control

1. Seeds soaked for an hour or so in paraffin before sowing are unpalatable and much less likely to be taken.

2. The mice can be trapped with nipper traps baited with chocolate.

Millipedes

There are many different types of millipedes, all have two pairs of legs on each segment (centipedes have one pair of legs per segment and should not be killed as they are beneficial). Most millipedes do no harm as they feed on dead plant material. One or two species become pests by feeding on seeds, stems and roots. Their distribution is patchy and they often occur in one part of a garden whilst being absent from another. If seedlings fail to emerge it is possible that millipedes are responsible, if so a search in the top few centimetres of soil will reveal 2cm (1in) long greyish brown millipedes with rather flattened bodies.

Control

1. Neglected gardens often have high millipede populations; regular cultivation and good garden hygiene gradually reduces the numbers.

2. Dusting with a contact insecticide will give some, but not complete, control.

3. Hand searching near to the damage and removing millipedes is effective where populations are small.

Moles

Moles do not eat plants, they feed almost exclusively on earthworms and other soil creatures. They make a series of tunnels fairly near to the surface and run through these at regular intervals to collect worms which have fallen in. Their tunnels when running under seedlings and other immature plants cause considerable damage. Molehills (the material removed during tunnel building) are also a nuisance. Moles tend to live singly and what appears to be a lot of damage may be the work of just one individual. However when that individual is removed another may move in to take his/her place especially in autumn when the young are dispersing.

Control

1. Trapping moles is quite easy as they use the same run many times. Traps are not set in molehills but in the tunnel between two molehills. The trap is placed in the tunnel and carefully covered to exclude any light. When the mole passes through the trap he springs it and is killed.

2. Other methods include child's windmills stuck in the ground to cause vibrations which the moles find unpleasant and electronic repellent devices.

Onion fly

Onion fly is very similar to the cabbage root fly except that it affects onions and leeks and not brassicas. Damage can occur at any time from May to September. The white larvae tunnel into the bulbs of onions; leeks and shallots but onions are more likely to be affected than the other two. Groups of young plants are killed and the tissues of older plants soften and rot. Onion fly is much less common than cabbage root fly.

Control

1. Remove and burn infested plants.

2. On gardens where onion fly occurs cover with fleece after sowing or planting.

3. Treat soil with a contact insecticide; only do this if the problem becomes serious.

Pea moth

This moth is responsible for the small caterpillars which are sometimes found eating one of the peas in a freshly opened pod. The adult moth lays its eggs on the plant and the tiny caterpillar bores into a pod. Once inside, it burrows into a single pea producing a lot of rather unpleasant frass.

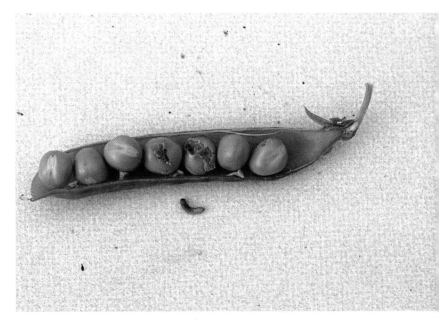

Pea moth

Control

1. The use of cloches and an early variety to produce a crop before the moths are flying is very effective.

2. Covering the row with fleece prevents the moths from laying. This is more difficult with the tall varieties.

3. Spray a contact pesticide for 10 days, beginning when the first flowers open. If the spray is applied in late evening there is less chance of killing pollinating insects and more chance of killing the pea moths. In areas where the populations of pea moth are high, spraying is only partially successful.

Rabbits

Rabbits can create havoc in the vegetable garden especially when plants are small. They find transplanted brassicas very pal-

Rabbit

atable and will destroy whole rows in a single night. The damage is easily identified; unlike birds the rabbit eats the main veins of the leaves as well as the leaf blades. The presence of the typical spherical droppings usually confirms the culprit.

Control

1. A dependable method of control is to fence the rabbits out of the garden with chicken wire. The bottom of the wire must be buried to prevent the rabbits from burrowing underneath.

2. Fleece, draped over plants will prevent rabbits from eating them.

3. It is legal to shoot or trap rabbits. On no account should snares be set as these cause the rabbits to suffer and may catch other animals.

Slugs and snails

These are one of the most difficult pests; there are several species some of which live entirely under the soil. They feed by rasping the vegetation away with a special 'tongue' which acts like a file. They feed on a very wide range of plants including potato tubers, celery, lettuce, brassicas and asparagus. They shelter under stones, debris and leaf litter during the day and feed at night. They remain active throughout the year and feed whenever the temperature is above freezing, Slugs and snails lay eggs in clusters of 10 – 30 in soil cavities.

Control

1. Traps consisting of half beer and half water set at soil level will drown many slugs although the largest species can crawl out of these.

2. Good garden hygiene reduces overall populations. A tidy garden has fewer places for them to hide from predators.

3. Encouraging frogs and toads into the garden (with a small pond) is a long term method which is very effective.

4. Poison baits laid strictly in accordance with the manufacturers' instructions will kill hundreds especially on a damp night. (Extra care must be taken as some baits are poisonous to animals and birds).

5. Biological control is available in the form of a clay which contains some 6,000,000

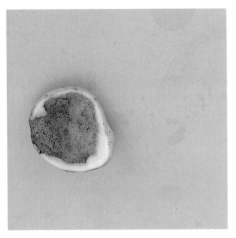

Above: Potato hollowed out by slugs

Left: Environmentally friendly insecticide in a very convenient pack

Below: Slug on melon

Right: Scarecrow

nematodes, this is available as 'Nemaslug' from Defenders Ltd or Natures Friends from garden centres. This is diluted and watered onto the plants and soil. The nematodes enter the slugs and breed; the slugs stop feeding and are eventually killed. This gives protection for about 6 weeks, after this time the nematodes disperse and slugs move into the cleared area from the untreated soil. Biological control is probably too expensive for extensive use in the vegetable garden.

6. Some varieties, like Pentland Squire potatoes, are fairly resistant to slugs, in contrast sweeter varieties like Maris Bard are very susceptible.

Wireworms

Wireworms are the larvae of the click beetle. They live deep in the soil for several years moving upwards to feed during spring and autumn. They have six tiny legs and are 1.5cm (¾in) long, segmented, shiny yellow and tough skinned. Wireworms feed on the underground parts of several vegetables by biting through the root; they also make narrow tunnels in potatoes.

Control

1. Wireworms usually live under grass land and are only troublesome for 2 or 3 years in a garden which was formed from old grassland. The best method of control is to avoid growing root crops and potatoes for the first 2 years. After this time the numbers will be considerably reduced and any damage will be slight.

2. If cultivated areas are kept weed-free the adult click beetles are less likely to lay eggs.

Basic Pest Control

❏ Accept a small amount of damage and only use chemicals if the yield is likely to be much reduced.
❏ Take extreme care when using chemicals, killing predators, parasites and pollinators is like shooting yourself in the foot!
❏ Good garden hygiene is essential. Avoid clutter and compost all organic waste.
❏ Practice crop rotation.
❏ Select resistant varieties where these are available.
❏ Control weeds especially during the autumn.
❏ Cover all brassicas with fleece after planting out.
❏ When peas begin to germinate cover them with fleece but watch out for mouse damage as they can get under the fleece.
❏ Reduce slugs with beer traps, encourage frogs and toads. Use slug baits with care.
❏ Delay sowing swedes until June.
❏ Visit your garden in the dark and seek pests with a torch. Place a barrier around carrots, do not 'store' carrots in the soil if root fly is present. Grow crops early in the season by raising the plants indoors and transplanting.

9
DISEASES OF VEGETABLES

There are many infectious diseases which people may catch; fortunately only a few of these are common. It is just the same with plants; there are plant diseases which most gardeners will never see and there are a few which are all too common.

A disease in a vegetable is caused by either a bacterium, a fungus or a virus. Disease organisms live in or on the plants, consuming their tissues and seriously reducing yields.

Bacteria

There are many millions of bacteria in each spadeful of soil; most of these make a living by converting dead material into fertilisers. One group of bacteria lives in swellings on pea and bean roots and converts air into nitrate fertiliser. A single individual is very small and it would take thousands to cover a pin head. When conditions are favourable [i e wet, warm and food] bacteria multiply at an alarming rate. Numbers increase by

Above: Bacteria entering wound on a custard white marrow

Above left: Bordeaux mixture

Rust on leeks

Organic gardeners' fungicide

individuals dividing into two; the new individuals repeat the process making four, and so on. Most bacterial diseases are wet and messy. They are secondary infections caused by bacteria invading damaged tissue.

Fungus

A fungus consists of a long thin thread, growing through the material that it is feeding upon. There are millions of miles of these threads in the soil helping to break down dead material into fertilisers. Sometimes the threads join together to form the fruiting bodies we see on moulds. Fungi reproduce by producing spores – 'seeds' so small that they float in the air, these are sometimes seen as a smoke when grey mould is disturbed. Spores are produced in very large numbers – a mature mushroom for example produces them at the rate of half a million a minute! Some fungi produce cysts that remain dormant in the soil for many years and only come to life when the host crop is planted again.

Whilst the vast majority of fungi feed on dead material and are harmless, a few cause diseases by feeding on living plants.

Virus

A virus is even smaller than a bacterium. Unlike bacteria and fungi a virus cannot survive for any length of time outside a living plant. They are passed from plant to plant by greenfly, whitefly, eelworm and possibly knives. Potato plants pass virus diseases from one year to the next in their seed tubers. 'Seed' potatoes are produced from healthy stock in those parts of the country where there are no greenfly. Where greenfly are present, home saved tubers all carry virus diseases.

As the virus lives inside the plant it is impossible to treat them with sprays. Prevention is the only 'cure' for virus diseases.

PREVENTING VEGETABLE DISEASES

Good husbandry

Plants have an inherited resistance to most diseases and they fight back. A weak plant is more likely to become diseased than a well grown one. The first line of defence is to heed the methods of good husbandry and grow good plants.

Crop rotation

Crop rotation is less successful in a garden than on a farm, as soil is more easily moved from one area to another, it travels on tools, boots and the roots of plants. In spite of this a regular 3 year rotation does keep several common diseases in check.

Strict garden hygiene

Dead crop material often carries disease and should be removed on a regular basis. Examples are: dead leaves on and under Brussels sprouts, lettuce running to seed, unharvested turnips and pea straw.

Weed control

Some diseases also infect weeds and live in them throughout the winter.

Purchasing top quality plant material

Some diseases are transmitted on seeds and other plant material. Purchases should always be made with care, seed potatoes for example carry several virus diseases and those on offer in shops will be certificated disease free. Gifts of seed potatoes grown by friends although well meaning may be disease ridden. Brassica plants are often traded and this is a common way of introducing clubroot. Only buy, or accept brassicas that have been pot grown in sterile compost.

Regular inspection

If you recognise the odd diseased plant, pull it up before it infects the others. Regular inspection means that chemical sprays will be applied at an early stage of infection when they are most effective.

Resistant varieties

Some varieties are more susceptible to disease then others; conversely some varieties are more resistant. Resistant varieties however can become infected and the use of these is an aid not a cure.

Raising plants inside & transplanting

Plants that have been raised with their own ball of sterile compost will grow away more strongly and be less affected by disease than those which are dug up from a seed bed.

Best sowing time

Seeds sown in wet, cold soil are at a susceptible stage for much longer than seeds sown in good conditions. There is nothing to be gained by putting seeds into cold soil, later sowings usually catch up.

Treating plants with care

This is particularly important when harvesting. Damaged potatoes for example are more likely to rot in store than those with their skins intact.

The use of chemical sprays

Chemical sprays can be very effective especially against fungus diseases – providing the infection is treated in its very early stages. The manufacturers' instructions must be strictly adhered to – it is food you are growing.

Common Vegetable Diseases

Crops affected	Symptoms	Disease	Control Methods	Spray?
Lettuce	Leaves yellow between veins	Beet western yellow veins	Remove and burn Control weeds	No
Potatoes Outdoor tomatoes	Brown patches on leaves Spreads quickly	Blight (a fungus not aphids)	Use new seed Garden hygiene	Fungicide before infection in hot damp weather
Parsnip	Black cracks in root. Root rots	Canker	Lime soil. Grow resistant variety	No
French beans Runner beans	Brown spots on leaves	Chocolate spot	Remove infected plants	Bordeaux mixture
Cabbage, Sprouts, Cauliflower	Plants wilt in sun growths on roots	Clubroot	Lime soil. Use pot grown plants Crop rotation	Dip bare root transplant in calomel
Courgettes Cucumbers Gherkins	Mottled yellow leaves, with some surface distortion	Cucumber mosaic virus	Destroy infected plants. Grow extra plants	No – but control aphids as they spread virus
All crops which are grown from seeds	Seedlings 'neck' and fall over	Damping off	Sow thinly. Avoid cold soil. Sow in sterile compost	Dust seeds with fungicide. Use Cheshunt
Brassicas Courgettes Lettuces Onions	Powdery spots on leaves. Onion leaves fall at point of infection	Downy mildew	Do not overcrowd. Use resistant varieties Crop rotation	Yes – with fungicide
Cucumbers Lettuces Tomatoes	'Smoking' grey mould. Lettuces rot at base and wilt	Grey mould (Botrytis)	Destroy infected plants or remove infected parts	Yes – with fungicide
Beans, Lettuces, Potatoes	Yellow spots and mottles on leaves	Mosaic virus	Remove and burn Disease is seed borne	No
Onions	Grey rot on necks of onions in store	Neck rot	Dry before storing. Remove infected parts	Dust sets with fungicide
Brassicas, Peas, Cucumbers	Powdery, white spots on leaves	Powdery mildew	Remove infected parts	Yes – fungicide at first sign
Peas, Beans	Plants shrivel Roots blacken	Root rot	Crop rotation Burn infected parts	Dress seeds with fungicide
Leeks	Orange blotches on leaves	Rust	Crop rotation Burn infected plants	No
Potatoes	Ragged, scabs on tubers	Scab	Do not lime. Water well	No
Turnips	Mosaics on leaves Growing tip dies	Turnip mosaic virus	Pull up affected and burn	No
Carrots	Purple roots	Violet root rot	Crop rotation	No

10
PLASTIC PROTECTION

Cloches

A cloche is a low transparent cover which is designed to protect large plants during the early stages of their growth and small plants from sowing to maturity. They come in all shapes and sizes. Some are expensive, rigid and easy to use whilst others are cheap, flimsy and time consuming.

A few good cloches are an excellent aid to the vegetable gardener and have the following uses:

❏ Warming the soil in early spring to bring forward sowing and planting dates.
❏ Help transplants to become established.
❏ Protect plants from birds, rabbits and some insects.
❏ Enable half hardy crops to be grown by protecting them during the early stages of growth.
❏ Protect from late spring frost.
❏ Harden off greenhouse grown plants.
❏ Covering parts of rows of salads to stagger maturity times.
❏ As a nursery area for brassica, lettuce and other plants.
❏ Extend the season into late autumn for parsley, lettuce etc.
❏ Protect some crops throughout the winter.

Limitations of cloches:

❏ The night temperature is only a degree or so above the outside temperature and plants can become frost damaged.
❏ Plants may become tender and may collapse when the cloche is removed.
❏ Leaves and growing points which are in contact with the plastic are sometimes damaged.
❏ With some types watering is difficult.
❏ Weed germination and growth is speeded up.

Cloche

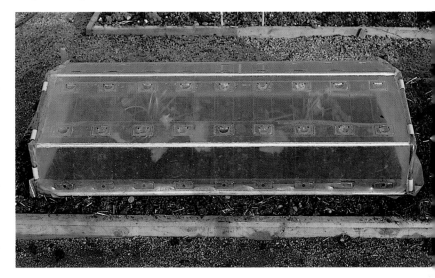

Above: Pepper

Above right: The board under the aubergine is to protect it from the soil

Points to remember when using cloches

When properly used, cloches are a real boon for vegetable growing – especially in the spring. To get full benefit from soil warming in spring, cloches must be in place for 2 weeks before sowing. Sudden removal should be avoided as plants may collapse in wind or sun. Some cloches are designed to allow for a gradual increase in ventilation but most are not. Plants can be gradually acclimatised to outside conditions (hardened off) by removing the cloches during the day and replacing them at night. In hot weather this may be preceded by removing the cloches for a few hours in the evening for 2 or 3 days.

Plastic Film Covers

The simplest and cheapest method of crop protection is a sheet of perforated or slitted plastic film, laid over the soil and held in position by burying the edges. This is an excellent method of warming the soil before sowing or planting. The seed bed does not dry out and germination time is reduced, this is particularly valuable with slow germinating vegetables like parsnips. The seedlings lift the sheet as they grow.

Removing the sheet however presents real problems, the crop is suddenly exposed to wind chill and low humidity. The more advanced the crop the greater the damage. Removal when the first true leaf is appearing is a good time especially if this coincides with dull wet weather.

Horticultural Fleece

Horticultural fleece is probably the vegetable gardeners' best aid for crop protection. Fleece is a fabric made from polypropylene. The polypropylene is stabilised against ultra violet light and formed into a mass of short threads. The threads are not woven together like normal cloth, but pressed together in a higgledy-piggledy fashion. The result is a very light material that can lie on top of plants without harming them. Plants grow well underneath as it admits light, air and water. The parts of plants which are in direct contact with the material do not become damaged as may happen with film.

Fleece is superior to plastic sheets because of its lightness and its ability to 'breathe'. Unlike plastic film, fleece need not be removed but can remain over the plants until they mature. In addition, plants protected by fleece are much less likely to suffer from the wind damage associated with films.

A fleece cloche is easily made by stapling a 2m (2yd) length between two roof laths the length of which is equal to the width of the fleece. The cloche is reduced or extended by winding or unwinding fleece around one of the laths. The laths are placed either side of a row and are usually heavy enough to prevent the fleece from blowing away. A peg or brick on the laths will only be necessary in very windy areas.

Apart from giving protection from the weather a fleece cloche placed over young cauliflower transplants protects them from: cabbage root fly, cabbage aphid, rabbits, pigeons, cabbage moth and cabbage butterflies.

Cold Frames

A cold frame is a low structure with a sloping glazed top, some frames also have glazed sides. In spring they are used to harden off greenhouse grown plants and to raise seedlings. In summer they are used for growing tender subjects like melons or cucumbers. In winter they are used to protect lettuce, parsley and other hardy crops. The glazed top may be of any transparent material, glass and polycarbonate are most often used. Glass is a little cheaper and gives a better greenhouse effect than polycarbonate, it is also more transparent. Polycarbonate is stronger and gives better insulation. When making a choice safety should also be considered – a child falling onto a glass cold frame does not bear thinking about.

The cold frame in the photograph has been raised on concrete blocks. This was done for a disabled gardener. Watering is easy and the plants are accessible, the space created underneath is useful for storage.

The Polytunnel

A polytunnel is an excellent aid to growing vegetables. Part of the tunnel in the photograph is organised into soil beds and used to produce early potatoes, cabbage, cauliflower, lettuce, radish, carrots and spinach; these are followed by tomatoes, cucumbers, peppers, aubergines, melons and sweetcorn. The other part of the tunnel has benches on which vegetable plants are raised for planting outside. (Bedding plants, many types of cuttings and flower crops are also grown). The growing season is extended by ten weeks, six in the spring and four in the autumn. There is no additional heating – with the exception of a small electric propagator. The polytunnel provides an excellent working environment – sheltered from wind and rain. It is however too hot for comfort on sunny summer afternoons.

A polytunnel consists of a framework of metal hoops, tied along the top to a metal ridgepole. The frame is covered with a sin-

Raised cold frame

gle sheet of polythene, secured to wooden door frames at each end. The sides of the sheet are either buried in the ground or fixed to metal grips. The atmosphere in a polytunnel is usually warmer and more humid than it is outside. There are more frost free days inside than outside and there are no winds or storms to damage plants. A polytunnel provides the ideal atmosphere in which to grow many types of vegetables; it also provides an ideal atmosphere for

Inside a polytunnel

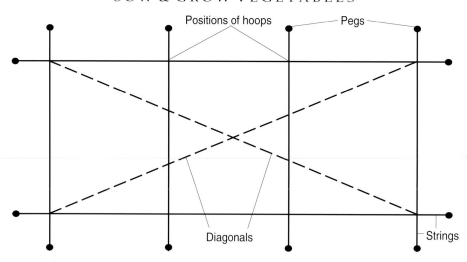

Positions of hoops　　Pegs

Diagonals　　Strings

Marking out a tunnel

some fungus diseases – particularly in the autumn. Red spiders and most insect pests can be controlled inside a tunnel by biological methods. Carrot fly, cabbage root fly and several other pests are no problem as the crops are usually harvested before these insects emerge. Slugs thrive in polytunnels but as birds and family pets can be kept outside, there are no environmental reasons why slug pellets should not be used.

A wide tunnel is better than a narrow one as a wide tunnel gives more working space away from the sides and ventilation is better. Side ventilation is available in most types but this is unnecessary for growing vegetables. Double doors or large vents at either end provide sufficient ventilation for tunnels up to 20m (60ft) long.

Modern polythene covers will last for 5 years before a replacement is needed. The best covers are stabilised to protect from ultra violet light and they trap solar radiation almost as well as glass. These covers are treated on the inside to spread condensation and so prevent drips. The cover for the 18ft by 40ft (approx 6m x 13m) tunnel in the photograph cost £70 and lasted for 6 years, this works out at less than £12 per year. This figure of £12 is very small when compared with the value of the produce and plants grown.

The modern polytunnel is designed to allow maximum headroom across the full width of the tunnel. The tunnel in the photograph allows a 6ft tall person to stand upright within 1yd of the side. This tunnel was manufactured by Fordingbridge (see reference section) who manufacture a full range of excellent tunnels for both amateurs and commercial growers.

A polytunnel is an excellent aid to vegetable production for the following reasons:

❏ Crops are produced 6 weeks before those grown outside.
❏ Some crops are available when they are expensive in the shops.
❏ Two crops are raised each year instead of one.
❏ Less hardy crops can be grown (eg peppers and aubergines).
❏ Yields of most vegetables are higher. The quality of many vegetables is better.
❏ Crops are not damaged by wind and storms.
❏ Fleece placed over plants to give extra protection does not blow away.
❏ Pests such as pigeons and rabbits are excluded.
❏ Cabbage root fly, carrot fly and other pests seldom enter a tunnel.
❏ Plants of most crops can be raised for

outside planting.
❏ The gardener becomes independent of the weather.

The disadvantages of a polytunnel are:

❏ Daily watering is necessary during the spring and summer months.
❏ Greenhouse pests such as white fly and red spider can be troublesome.
❏ More skill is required to grow crops in a tunnel than outside.
❏ The outside appearance is not very aesthetic (good looking).

Erecting a Polytunnel
Polytunnels are usually supplied in kit form and the erection is easy for the average handy person, but four people are needed to attach the cover. After the tunnel has arrived the first job is to lay out and identify all the parts.

Siting
Ideally the ridge of a polytunnel should run west to east, in this way the longest side will get sun all day. There are other considerations, the siting of a polytunnel will depend upon the garden layout and design – it is a matter of 'Where will it fit?' rather than 'Where is south?'

Marking out the base
1. Using two pegs and a length of string mark the position of the tunnel side. Drive the pegs in 1yd beyond each end of the tunnel.
2. Mark the other side and the two ends in the same way, squaring the corners with a rectangle of wood.
3. Measure both diagonals, if the measurements are not exactly the same, the base is not square.
4. If necessary adjust the corners until the diagonals are exactly the same length.
5. Mark the positions of the ends of intermediate hoops with pegs and string. The distances between the hoops should be equal.

6. Leave the pegs where they are and re move the strings.
7. Dig the holes.
8. Fill the holes with concrete and replace the strings. Position the tubes so that their centres are underneath the point where the strings cross.
9. Using a long straight plank and a spirit level check that the tops of the tubes are level; drive in any which are proud. (Note: protect the top of the tube with a board before hitting with a hammer).

Raised flower border to improve appearance of a polytunnel

Onions protected from wind damage with horticultural fleece

A fleece cloche

an *anti-fogging agent, make sure you put it on the right way up.

3. When pulling the sheet taut, take care not to stretch it.
4. Fix the sheet as tight as possible along the length of the ridge, before attaching it to the sides. (The final appearance of the tunnel depends upon this).

* an anti-fogging treatment causes droplets of condensation to spread into a thin film. This allows more light in and improves insulation.

There are other designs of polytunnel, one of which can be lifted and moved. This type of tunnel could be moved from tomatoes to chrysanthemums and then on to grow an early crop of vegetables before being used once again for tomatoes.

Using a polytunnel

Anyone who can grow vegetables outside can grow them in a polytunnel. Vegetables are grown in soil (preferably on raised beds) in the same way as they are outside except that they are sown or planted **6 weeks earlier** than outside and they require regular watering. The other major difference is that two crops are grown in the same area instead of one. The cropping plan depends upon the needs of the gardener's family. Sound soil management, including crop rotation and generous manuring is important in a polytunnel.

Ventilation

Good ventilation is provided by opening doors or vents at both ends of a polytunnel. Apart from cold spells in the depth of winter one end (or more usually both) is opened every day. This is most important in autumn when conditions become favourable for grey mould and other fungus diseases. On sunny days which are followed by frosty nights the tunnel should be given full ventilation, it should be closed up before the sun goes down in order for the sheet to get a layer of condensation, this

After the concrete has set the sequence of erection is as follows:

1. Slide the hoops into position.
2. Fix the ridgepole with the brackets provided but do not tighten any nuts.
3. Adjust the hoops so they are all exactly in line with each other and at right angles to the ridgepole.
4. Tighten all nuts.
5. Fix the door frames (these are usually wooden).
6. Cover all nuts and sharp edges with tape.
7. Stick anti-hotspot tape over the outside of the hoops. (Anti-hotspot tape is exceptionally smooth which helps the positioning of the sheet; it also extends the life of a polythene cover by at least one year).

Covering the Tunnel.

Different manufacturers have different methods of fixing the sheet. Points to remember are:

1. Wait for a calm day as the slightest breeze makes a cover unmanageable. The air is most still at dawn and this is often a suitable time to cover the frame.
2. If the plastic is treated on one side with

layer freezes and helps to insulate the inside.

Temperature

A polytunnel warms by the greenhouse effect and there is no chill factor from the wind. It is unheated and the temperature inside will fall below freezing. Tender crops such as early potatoes are best covered with fleece, this will not need anchoring as there is no wind to blow it away. In very cold spells a body blanket (aluminium foil) is used as a second cover during night time only.

In summer a polytunnel can become very hot even when doors and vents are fully open. Plants withstand these high temperatures providing they are well watered.

Water

A polytunnel needs a good reliable water supply. Ideally in summer a hose pipe is used for watering, care must be taken not to damage the soil structure.

Vegetables which are unsuitable for a polytunnel

The following list of vegetables are not suitable for polytunnel production for a variety of reasons. The ones marked with * should be raised in a polytunnel and then transplanted outside.

Artichokes, Asparagus, *Broad beans, *Brussels sprouts, *Cabbage (not Hispi), *Sprouting broccoli, *Celeriac, *Celery, Garlic, *Kale, *Leeks, Parsnip, Maincrop potatoes, *Runner beans, *Onions, Salsify, Shallots, Swede.

All the other vegetables listed in this book will produce excellent crops inside the polytunnel.

Note: Plants which are raised in a polytunnel must be hardened off before they are planted in the garden.

A polytunnel needs double doors to give good ventilation

Polytunnel – this type can be lifted and moved

11
VEGETABLES

ARTICHOKES, GLOBE
Cynara scolymus

This plant does not appear in the wild, it is an edible thistle which may have been developed from the cordoon. It is widely grown in Italy and France, yields are low in the U.K. where it is often grown as a decorative plant in the flower border. The plant is a short lived perennial which needs replacing every 4 or 5 years. Although fairly hardy some protection may be needed in winter.

Two parts of the plant are edible, the young blanched shoots and the flower buds. The white shoots are used in salads and the flower buds are boiled. The tips of the flower bud scales are too tough to eat and the florets (the 'choke') are also inedible.

Soil
A good fertile soil with a pH of 6.5, in a sheltered sunny site is necessary for a worthwhile crop. The main requirement being plenty of organic matter to provide nutrients and to retain moisture. As with all permanent plantings, bone meal at the rate of 450g per sq m (1lb sq yd) should be worked into the soil.

Sowing and Planting
Globe artichokes are easily grown from seeds sown in heat in February, these will produce a crop of three or four buds late in the season. Plants from seeds are rather variable and it is better to propagate from named varieties. Purchased plants are planted out in spring and the beds remain productive for three or four years. New beds are established by taking suckers (sideshoots) from an established bed in April and planting them up.

Spacing
Depending upon the size and shape of the bed, globe artichokes are either planted 60cm (2ft) along rows which are 120 cm (4ft) apart or 90cm (3ft) apart along rows that

Artichoke

Grower's Timetable – GLOBE ARTICHOKES

Creating a bed

Autumn	Prepare the soil by deep digging and mixing in organic matter at the rate of 5 to10kg per sq m (10 - 20lb per sq yd) and bone meal at the rate of 450g per sq m (1lb per sq yd).
April	Purchase plants and plant firmly. Space the plants 90cm (3ft) apart, along rows which are 90cm (3ft) apart. Summer Water as necessary. Control weeds.
Autumn	Harvest any flower buds before they open.
Late Autumn	Tidy up the bed by removing dead leaves.
Winter	Protect from severe frost with straw or leaves.

Looking after an established bed

April	Apply a general purpose fertiliser (eg Growmore at the rate of 80g per sq m 3oz per sq yd) or a mulch of well rotted compost.
Summer	Control weeds.
Autumn	Harvest the flower buds when plump but before they open. The terminal bud will be ready first. If very large artichokes are wanted, remove the side buds when they are 2cm (1in) in diameter. These may be eaten whole.
Late Autumn	Tidy up the bed by removing dead leaves and stems.
Winter	Protect from severe frost with straw or leaves.

are also 90 cm (3ft) apart.

Fertilising

A general purpose fertiliser (eg Growmore at the rate of 80g per sq m 3oz per sq yd) or a mulch of well rotted compost is applied in early spring.

Watering

During the first summer the young plants require regular waterings of up to 10 litres per sq m (2gal per sq yd) every week, depending upon rainfall. Established beds do not require watering unless the summer is exceptionally dry.

Harvest.

The buds are cut off with a sharp knife when they are fully formed but before the flower opens. The second crop, which grows from sideshoots, is harvested when the buds are the size of a very small hen's egg. The small buds are usually sliced, fried and eaten as a second vegetable.

Star Variety

Violetto di Chioggia
The most suitable for the U.K. climate.

Cooking

Cut off the stem and 2cm (1in) across the tops of the leaves. Trim the side leaves with scissors. Tie a slice of lemon on the bottom of each bud with string. Simmer in boiling, salted water until the bottom of the bud is tender (about 25 minutes). Remove the centre of the artichoke, scrape away all of the furry inside and replace the centre upsidedown. Reheat in boiling water for a couple of minutes, drain and serve.

ARTICHOKES, JERUSALEM

Helianthus tuberosus

This North American plant is very similar to the sunflower except that its leaves are smaller and it only flowers in exceptionally hot summers.

It is grown for the tubers which look like knobbly potatoes. The carbohydrate in Jerusalem artichokes is more suitable for diabetics than the one in potatoes. Nicknamed 'fartichokes', they can have an antisocial effect upon the digestive system.

Jerusalem artichokes are up to 3m (10ft) tall and are a quick and easy way of forming a summer screen or windbreak. Jerusalem artichokes are very hardy and extremely easy to grow.

Soil

Jerusalem artichokes will grow in virtually any soil but well-manured clay soils yield the heaviest crops.

Planting

Jerusalem artichokes are grown from tubers, these can be purchased or home saved from the previous year. A hole is dug at each station deep enough to allow about 8cm (3in) of soil over the tuber.

Spacing

The tubers are spaced 40cm (16in) apart along the row. Rows are spaced 90cm (3ft) apart.

Fertiliser

Jerusalem artichokes have a high phosphate requirement; however additional fertiliser is unnecessary in a well-managed garden soil.

Watering

Tubers form as the days become shorter, one or two waterings of 22 litres per sq m (4 gal per sq yd) in a dry August which follows a dry summer will enhance yield.

Support

Jerusalem artichokes have strong stems that may blow over in high winds. A post at each end of the row with strings tied either side will prevent this.

Harvest

Harvesting begins in autumn and continues throughout the winter, as and when tubers are required. In areas where the ground is likely to become frozen hard the tubers may be stored, a high humidity and temperatures near to freezing will keep them in good condition. The tubers are thin skinned and very easily damaged. The whole plant is dug up and the tubers carefully picked from the bottom of the stem. Tubers which are left in the ground will grow the following year and may become a nuisance.

Star Variety

Fuseau
Smooth skinned and much less knobbly than the common types.

Cooking

Wash and peel the tubers and place them in a pan, barely cover with water and add a little salt. Simmer until tender, drain and serve.

Grower's Timetable – JERUSALEM ARTICHOKES	
March	Using a trowel, plant each tuber with a covering of 8cm (3in) of soil.
May	Earth up by drawing soil over the plants from each side of the row.
Summer	Hoe when necessary to control weeds. On windy sites, drive a stake into the ground at each end of the row. Tie strings between the stakes at either side of the row at a height of 120cm (4ft).
Autumn and Winter	Harvest as required. Save tubers for next year's crop.
Spring	Fork over the area and remove any tubers (or parts of tubers) left in the ground.

4 year and 1 year old asparagus crowns

ASPARAGUS
Asparagus officinalis

This plant grows wild on the coastal areas of Europe and has been in use for over 2,000 years both as a medicine and as a food. The young shoots are edible; these are usually eaten green but may be blanched and eaten white.

An asparagus plant is either male or female; the male plants are more productive than the females. The seeds from female plants produce seedlings that can ruin a good bed. It is far better therefore to have a bed that contains only male plants.

Soil

Asparagus is likely to remain in the same position for 20 years or more, the site must therefore be carefully chosen and the soil extremely well prepared. What is required is a deep, weed free, well drained, moisture retentive soil with a pH of more than 6.5. The majority of gardens will not be able to provide all these conditions. Light, well drained soils could be used by incorporating lots of organic matter and then mulching regularly. Acid soils can be corrected by the application of lime over a period of around 18 months and perennial weeds can be cleared with herbicides. Gardeners with clay, poorly drained and other unsuitable soils

can grow good asparagus by means of a very deep bed. The deep bed will project 1m (1yd) above the surface and be filled with sandy soil mixed with lots of decaying organic matter. The standard 120cm (4ft) wide bed allows for two rows of asparagus.

Sowing and Planting

Asparagus is easily raised from April sown seeds. Seeds produce both male and female plants and it is not possible to distinguish one from the other until they flower. The females have berries. Asparagus is usually grown by planting crowns; a crown consists of the roots and dormant buds of a single plant.

The best way of establishing an asparagus bed is to purchase one year old, all male crowns from a reputable supplier. Cheap and 'special offer' crowns should never be purchased. When the crowns arrive they should be unpacked immediately and planted as soon as possible, if the surface of the crowns appears dry they are soaked for a couple of hours before planting. A flat bottomed trench 22cm (9in) wide and 10cm (4in) deep is dug; the crowns are placed buds uppermost in the bottom of the trench with the roots spread out like the spokes of a wheel. The trench is then carefully backfilled.

Spacing.

Close spacing increases the yield but makes the spears thinner, wide spacing gives a reduced yield of thicker spears. A good compromise is to space the rows 60cm (2ft) apart with the crowns spaced 35cm (14in) apart down the row. The distances are measured from the centres of the crowns and not from the tips of the roots.

Fertilising

Asparagus is a maritime plant and responds to a dressing of salt; table salt can be applied in early spring at the rate of 50g per sq m (2oz sq yd). A liberal mulch of well-rotted

manure or compost should be applied each summer after the final harvest. If mulching material is in short supply 80g per square metre (3oz per sq yd) of a general purpose fertiliser should be given in early March.

Bed Maintenance

The asparagus bed must be kept weed free; the bed may be ruined if perennial weeds (see page 41) become established. Seedling weeds which germinate can be controlled by light hoeing, the odd dandelion, dock or thistle that appears should be carefully removed with a handfork, root and all. The summer mulching will reduce the need for weeding.

If couch grass invades an established asparagus bed it can be controlled with the herbicide Dalapon. Dalapon is applied in spring before the spears begin to grow or in summer after the ferns have developed. If contact with the ferns is avoided the couch will be killed and the asparagus left unharmed.

Green ferns feed the roots that store the materials for next year's crop, if green ferns are cut the yield will be reduced. When ferns begin to turn brown in autumn they are cut off at ground level and removed.

Harvesting

It takes 2 years for an asparagus plant to become properly established and lay down enough reserves to produce rapid growth the following spring. This rapid growth forms the crop so there is **no harvest during the first or second year.**

Asparagus is harvested by cutting off all spears (including any thin ones) just below soil level as soon as they are 12cm (5in) high. The first year a bed is cropped, harvesting ceases the second week of May, in subsequent years harvesting continues until the end of May. Spears which form after this time are left to grow into fern.

Star Varieties

Lucullus
Only available as male crowns.

Connovers colossal
The best variety to grow from seeds.

Cooking

Wash the spears and trim the bottom of the stems. Tie the spears in a neat bundle with two pieces of string and wrap a strip of foil around the middle. Stand upright in a 4cm (1in) of salted, boiling water and simmer until the tops are just tender. Lift out, remove the foil and string, drain and serve.

Alternative method: Lay the spears in a shallow dish with a little water, partially cover the dish and cook on the high setting in a microwave oven. Purpose made asparagus steamers are available from kitchen shops.

Grower's Timetable – ASPARAGUS

Creating a bed
1. Check the pH, if this is below 6.8 add lime. About 450g per sq m (1lb per sq yd) of ground limestone is needed to raise the pH by one point, eg from 5 to 6. If the pH is below 5.5 liming should be spread over two seasons.
2. In autumn double dig the area mixing in between 5kg and 10kg per sq m (10 to 20lb per sq yd) of fairly dry well-rotted manure or compost.
3. In spring make trenches 22cm (9in) wide, 10cm (4in) deep and 60cm (2ft) apart.
4. Soak the crowns for 2 hours in water.
5. Place the crowns buds uppermost in the bottom of the trench 35cm (14in) apart with the roots spread out like the spokes of a wheel. Carefully refill the trench.
6. During the summer water in dry weather and keep the bed free of all weeds.
7. When the ferns turn brown in autumn, use secateurs to cut them off at ground level.

Looking after an established bed

March:	Apply 80g per sq m (3oz per sq yd) of a general purpose fertiliser (Growmore or similar).
	Sprinkle 50 g per square metre (2oz sq yd) of cooking salt over the bed.
April and May	Harvest the spears regularly as they reach a height of 12cm (5in) by cutting off with a sharp knife, just below soil level.
July	Control weeds throughout the summer and autumn.
	Apply a mulch of organic matter.
October	Cut off and remove all the ferns after they have turned brown.

BEETROOT

Beetroot was bred from a wild species which grows on the seashores of Europe (including the British Isles). Although beetroot is most often eaten cold as a salad it is also delicious as a hot vegetable.

Beetroot is fairly hardy but young plants are sensitive to cold, bolting may occur if a period of cold weather coincides with this sensitive period. Bolting plants produce a flower spike instead of a root and are quite useless. Plant breeders have attempted to produce non-bolting varieties and have had a measure of success, particularly with the varieties Avonearly, Monodet and Boltardy. A 'non-bolting' variety should be selected for the earliest sowings. The newer varieties also have increased sweetness and a flesh which is free from white rings. A mature flower of beetroot consists of a cluster of two or three seeds covered with a corky material, when sown each cluster will produce several seedlings. 'Rubbed' or 'monogerm' seeds are obtainable and these produce single seedlings.

Beetroot are often classified according to the shape of the roots, the small spherical varieties are usually grown for early crops and the larger tapered roots as maincrop and storage varieties. The cylinder shape varieties are favoured by some cooks as they slice into even sized rings.

Soil
Beetroot can be grown in most soils but the ideal is well drained and humus rich with a pH between 6.5 and 7.5.

Sowing
The soil is raked to a medium tilth and seeds are sown in rows 10 to 20mm (½ - ¾ in) deep.

Spacing
For maincrop, rows are 30cm (12in) apart and seedlings thinned to 15cm (6in) apart. If baby beet are

Top picture: Varieties of beetroot

Lower picture: Twisting the tops off

required, the seeds are sown very thinly and not thinned. Beets are harvested by gently rotating them as soon as they are large enough and the others left to grow.

Fertiliser

Top dress between the rows with 70g per sq metre (2oz per sq yd) of Nitrate of Soda after the seeds have germinated. As beetroot is a maritime plant it responds to the sodium in this type of fertiliser. If other types of nitrogen fertiliser (or no fertiliser) are used, sprinkle a little cooking salt alongside each row.

Watering

Too much water is bad for beetroot as it tends to increase leaf growth rather than root size. In very dry weather, prevent the soil from drying out by watering every 2 weeks. Do not soak the whole of the ground, just water alongside each row.

Harvest

Harvest by loosening the soil with a fork and gently pulling up the roots. Remove the tops immediately by twisting them off, this is better than using a knife as it reduces the sap loss from the wounds. Handle with extreme care as damaged roots soon begin to rot.

Storage

In mild districts, beetroot may be left in the ground and pulled as required. In other districts unwashed roots store well in polythene sacks kept in a cold but frost free shed.

Star Varieties

Boltardy
Bolt resistant, good colour and free from white rings.

Forono
Cylindrical roots, good cropper, susceptible to bolting therefore sow in May.

Grower's Timetable for an Early Crop – BEETROOT

1. In February select a non-bolting variety.
2. Fill a sectioned seedtray with multipurpose compost and water it.
3. Sow two seed clusters (or five monogerm seeds) in each section.
4. Keep in a warm room (or propagator) until germination occurs.
5. Transfer the tray to a greenhouse or cold frame and water as necessary.
6. When the soil outside begins to warm (March or April according to season and district) remove each clump of seedlings from the tray and plant out as clumps, the same depth as they were in the tray. Allow 15cm (6in) between each clump and 30cm (12in) between the rows.
7. Cover with cloches.
8. When the roots are large enough to eat, harvest the largest by gently rotating between fingers and thumb. This will leave the smaller roots to develop.

Growing the Maincrop

Make two more sowings of an early variety, one in May and one in June, to keep a succession of fresh tender roots. Make a single sowing of a globe variety in late May to be lifted for storing in October.

BORECOLE – see Kale

BROAD BEAN
Vicia faba
Broad beans have been cultivated for many thousands of years and are no longer found in the wild. The plants are very hardy and one

variety (Aquadulce) will overwinter from a November sowing in the milder parts of the country. **Sowings made after the end of April are unlikely to produce a very satisfactory crop.**

Broad beans are insect pollinated and should not be sprayed with insecticide whilst flowering as pollinating insects may be killed. Although it is usual to eat the seeds, very young pods can be eaten whole in the same way as French beans. The tops of the plants can also be harvested and eaten as a green vegetable.

Soil

Broad beans benefit from a deeply worked soil. Any pH between 5.5 and 7.0 is satisfactory.

Watering

Broad beans are unlikely to require any watering during the early stages of growth , indeed water at this stage can be harmful, by producing leaves at the expense of flowers and pods. Water is most effective when the plants begin to flower and when the beans begin to swell. Watering during dry weather at these times will increase the yield.

Unless the plants begin to wilt, do not water before the first flowers begin to open. When the first flowers appear give 10 litres per sq m (2gal per sq yd) and repeat this when the pods begin to swell. Apply the water directly to the base of the plants. In dry seasons water each week during the fruiting period.

Support

With the exception of very short varieties (egThe Sutton) broad beans require some support. Beans in raised beds can be supported by growing through a horizontal net

set 30cm (1ft) below their final height.

Beans in rows are easily supported by stretching two horizontal strings along both sides of the row. The strings are supported by garden canes at each end, if the row is long intermediate canes will be required.

Removing Tops

Black bean aphid is a serious pest of broad beans. The aphids begin feeding at the topmost growing point and increase in numbers at an alarming rate. The infestation then moves down to the flower buds and young fruits, these fail to develop and the crop is either lost or very much reduced. Ants feed on aphid secretions and run up and down the plants to collect this food. At the first sign of ants the tops of the plants should be removed. This will remove the winged aphids and help to prevent an early infestation. Aphids which fly in later are less likely to succeed as the most favourable feeding areas have been removed.

Harvest

Broad beans are best picked young and certainly before the skins

around the seeds mature and become tough. The connection between seed and pod should be soft, if the scar on the bean is black the bean has been left on the plant too long and the bean will be coarse with a tough skin.

If dry beans are required, leave the pods on the plant until they dry and turn black. These can then be harvested, shelled and the beans stored dry until required.

Star Variety

Witkiem Manita Masterpiece

Cooking

Drop into a small amount of lightly salted, boiling water and simmer until just tender.

Freezing

Broad beans freeze exceptionally well. Place in boiling water and blanch for one minute, cool immediately in cold water. Spread thinly on metal trays and freeze. When frozen transfer the beans to a storage container. Only freeze young, tender beans – if tough beans go into the freezer, tough beans will come out!

Removing the top from broad beans

Horizontal net to support broad beans

Grower's Timetable for an Early Crop – BROAD BEANS	
November	Sow the variety Aquadulce claudia in early November in a well drained soil. OR – (this method is recommended as better flavoured varieties can be grown)
February	Sow seeds 5cm (2in) deep individually in 7cm (3in) pots or deep root trainers using a general purpose compost. Keep in a warm room until the first seedlings can be seen breaking the surface.
March	Transfer to a cold greenhouse or cold frame. Water as necessary.
April	When the plants are 15cm (6in) high plant them out in double rows 22cm (9in) apart with 22cm (9in) between the rows. Allow 45 cm (18in) between each double row. Continue from ❏ as for the maincrop below..
Growers' Timetable for a Maincrop	
March	As soon as the ground begins to warm and when soil conditions allow, sow seeds 5cm (2in) deep and 11cm (4.5in) apart. Sow in double rows, 22cm (9in) apart with 45cm (18in) between each double row.
❏ April	Control weeds by regular, shallow hoeing with a dutch hoe. When the plants are about 30cm (1ft) high arrange the supports.
June	Harvest the young pods soon after they fill.
July	Pull up and compost plants as soon as the harvest is finished.
Note:	Sideshoots often grow after the main harvest, in some seasons a small late crop can be harvested, this crop is seldom worthwhile and it is better to use the ground for endive, radish, chinese cabbage or other quick maturing plants.

Brussels sprouts before and after removing the leaves

BROCCOLI
– see Calabrese

BRUSSELS SPROUTS
Brassica oleracae

A single stemmed biennial grown for its buds which resemble very small cabbages. Brussels sprouts were developed from the wild cabbage in Belgium during the 1800s and soon became an important vegetable in the colder areas of Europe. Some varieties are very hardy and can withstand temperatures as low as -10 °C (14°F). It is claimed that low temperatures improve the flavour, for this reason some gardeners do not begin picking until after the first autumn frosts. By careful choice of three different varieties it is possible to harvest sprouts from early September until April.

Sowing and Planting

Brussels sprouts are most often grown from transplants raised in a seed bed. It is however better to raise the plants in a cold greenhouse in either pots or root trainers. Pot grown plants have good root systems and withstand the shock of transplanting better than bare root plants. Pot grown plants are also better able to withstand clubroot.

The Brussels sprout bed is prepared well in advance to give the soil time to settle, as this crop grows best in a firm soil. In common with other brassicas Brussels sprouts are transplanted before the top of the stems become as thick as a pencil. Planting is done in late May and early June, the early varieties being planted first. Pressure with the foot alongside each plant firms the soil and makes a useful depression in which to apply water.

Where space is short, planting in between rows of early potatoes is sometimes practiced.

Space

Brussels sprouts required for regular picking need a lot of space - 90cm (35in) between the plants and the same distance between the rows. Sprouts grown for a single picking are planted 50cm x 50cm (20in).

Fertilising

Soil managed by the methods described in Chapter 1 will supply sufficient phosphorous and potassium. Brussels sprouts have a high nitrogen requirement and this is applied in two top dressings. The first is given soon after the plants have become established and the second six weeks later; the rate for each of these dressings is 100g of 10% nitrogen per sq m (33oz per sq yd). After the fertiliser is spread a rose can be used to give the soil a light watering.

Water

Transplants should always be watered in and, depending upon the season, may require watering two or three more times. Once the plants are well-established Brussels sprouts will only require watering during exceptionally dry summers.

Support

Brussels sprouts are tall plants that often fall over in autumn and winter especially in light soils and on windy sites. This can be prevented by pushing a strong 1m (1yd) garden cane into the soil as near to the base of the plant as possible. A piece of nylon string is used to secure the stem near to the top of the cane. Staking is done in late summer before the plants go over, otherwise considerable root disturbance results.

Harvest

The lowest sprouts develop first and are removed from the stem by sidewards pressure with the thumb. The smaller sprouts higher up the stems are left to develop, individual plants often produce sprouts over a period of 3 months. As the bottom leaves die off they are removed on a regular basis as normal garden hygiene and disease control. Towards the end of the season the top of each plant resembles a small cabbage, these can be harvested and used.

Pigeon Problems

In areas where pigeons are a nuisance it may be necessary to harvest the whole crop at a single picking and freeze it. In order to do this it is necessary to have all the buttons ready for picking at the same time. This is achieved by removing the top growing point when the bottom sprouts have a diameter somewhere between 6mm (¼in) and 12mm (½in). The top must be pinched out by 30 September in order to allow enough growing weather for the sprouts to form.

Star Varieties

Early: Peer Gynt
Mid season: Odette
Late: Fortress
    (not suitable for stopping)

Cooking

The loose outside leaves are removed. Two cuts in the form of a cross are made into the base of the stem about a quarter of the way into the sprout to allow even cooking. The sprouts are dropped into slightly salted boiling water and simmered until tender. A sharp knife is inserted into the thickest part of the sprout to test for tenderness. Brussel sprouts are delicious when steamed.

Freezing

The buttons are prepared as described for cooking before blanching for 2 minutes in boiling water. They are drained and plunged into cold water and left to cool for 2 or 3 minutes. After draining for a second time they are spread thinly on a metal tray and placed in the coldest part of the freezer. Once frozen the sprouts are transferred to a plastic container.

Grower's Timetable – BRUSSELS SPROUTS	
March/Early April:	Sow seeds 20mm (¾in) deep in a greenhouse or sow in a seed bed. Prepare a firm soil bed.
May:	Transplant into rows with the following distances apart: If required for regular picking: 90cm between the rows and 90cm (35in) between the plants. If required for a single picking: 50cm between the rows and 50cm (20in) between the plants. Water transplants in and (in dry weather) water again until established. Protect from cabbage root fly. (page 48)
June:	When the plants are established and beginning to grow, top dress with 100g per sq metre of 10% Nitrogen. Control weeds by shallow hoeing as necessary.
July:	Repeat the nitrogen dressing 6 weeks later. Cover with fleece from mid-summer, or remove caterpillars by hand.
August/September:	Stake each plant with a garden cane and tie.
Autumn/Winter:	Pick sprouts as required. Remove dead leaves throughout the harvest period.

CABBAGE
Brassica oleracea

This important crop originated along the shores of the Mediterranean Sea where the wild plants still grow. The ancient Greeks grew cabbage as a herb which they used for medical treatments. The cabbage is a very hardy biennial that is grown as an annual for its edible leaves and its very large terminal bud – the heart.

Types

Cabbage can be divided into three groups:

Spring Cabbage – sown end of July to beginning of August for harvest from April to June.

Summer Cabbage – sown February/March for harvest from June to October.

Winter cabbage – sown May for harvest from November to March.

Spring cabbages stand the winter as small plants, before growing away in early spring to form hearts in May/June. The sowing date for spring cabbage is critical and varies a little according to district. If sown too soon the plants bolt and if sown too late they are unable to survive the winter. In the Midlands the 20 July is about right, a week or so earlier in the north and a week or two later in the south according to local climate. These sowings produce plants large enough for transplanting from mid-September to early October. Spring cabbages are close planted to allow unhearted leafy plants to be harvested, whilst every third plant is left to develop a heart.

The groups are further subdivided according to heart shape, leaf texture and colour. These divisions are rather blurred at the edges, but in general, varieties of summer and winter cabbage produce round hearts whilst spring cabbages usually have pointed hearts. Cabbages have fairly smooth leaves but one group of winter cabbage – the savoys – has very crinkled leaves. Cabbage leaves are various shades of green or red but the inner hearts become blanched and very pale. The red coloured cabbages are often reserved for pickling, there is no reason why they cannot be eaten in the same way as other cabbage.

Soil

Cabbage will grow in any fertile soil with a pH between 5.5 and 7.0. Cabbage (including the other brassicas) should not be grown more often than one year in three as a precaution against the disease 'clubroot'. If this disease is present (and it usually is!) satisfactory brassicas can be grown by liming the soil and using transplants with a good root ball. Note: Wallflowers are also subject to clubroot, if these plants are raised in the vegetable garden they should be grown in the same rotation as the other brassicas.

Sowing

Cabbages are almost always transplanted. Seeds are sown in short rows 2cm (¾in) deep, in a small plot set aside for this purpose. The seedlings are kept weed free and transplanted before the stems are pencil thickness. A better method is to raise the plants individually in pots or root trainers in a cold greenhouse or cold frame. Refer to the chart on page 74 for sowing dates.

Spacing

Closely spaced cabbages produce smaller heads than those with plenty of space. Spacing therefore varies with the demands of the kitchen and the variety being used. Recommended spacings are given in the chart on page 74.

Fertilising

Summer and winter cabbage only achieve maximum yields when well supplied with nitrogen. Their high nitrogen requirement is met by applying 125g per sq m (3oz per sq yd) of 10% nitrogen fertiliser before planting. Six weeks later a similar amount is applied as a top dressing. In dry weather wash the fertiliser in with a light watering through a rose can. Spring cabbages receive only one application of nitrogen, given as a top dressing in spring when the plants begin to grow. The harvesting period can be extended by top dressing only one half of the plot and treating the other half 2 weeks later.

Cabbage will split if left too long before harvesting

Watering
If the soil is dry at sowing time soak the bottom of the drill before sowing. Transplants, especially bare

root ones, need a daily watering of 140ml (¼ pint) per plant – applied directly to the base of the plant.

Summer cabbages respond to watering by increasing their size. Plants which are watered each week grow to twice the size of unwatered ones. However a single watering 2 weeks before harvest produces a 65% size increase. This single watering gives a much better return for water and labour than regular watering. Water should be applied at the rate of 22 litres per square metre (4 gal per sq yd), any less will not be fully effective and any more may cause the heads to burst.

Harvest
Cabbages are harvested when the hearts are firm, this is tested by gently pressing the top of the heart with the finger tips. The whole cabbage is pressed over sideways with one hand to expose the stem whilst the other hand cuts through the stem with a sharp knife. Leaving a few leaves on the stalk and cutting a cross on the top, results in a further crop of small cabbages.

Succession
By correct choice of varieties and sowing dates it is possible to have hearted cabbages available throughout the year. The most likely month for a gap in supply is June, the best way to fill this gap is to sow the variety Hispi in a heated propagator in a cold greenhouse in February and plant out under cloches in April. Hispi cabbage is very quick maturing but it does not stand well and quickly runs to seed.

Cloches, or other forms of protection can be used to advance both spring and summer cabbage.

Star Varieties.
(listed in order of maturity)

Spring Cabbage
Avon Crest – used for spring greens or left to heart. Good resistance to bolting.
Durham Early – the best variety for greens.

Summer Cabbage
Hispi – see above.
Spitfire – pointed heads which stand longer than Hispi.
Golden Cross – round solid hearts which will stand for three months.
Minicole – Small oval heads, very long standing.
Ruby Ball – a red cabbage with a round heart.
Freshma – Dark oval heads, matures in October.

Winter Cabbage
Wirosa – a savoy type of excellent quality.
January King – dark green hearts tinged with purple.
Tundra – Solid white hearts, stands until April – excellent for coleslaw.

Cooking
Shred the cabbage finely and either steam or boil. To boil: Drop into boiling salted water. Simmer with the lid off until tender and then drain. In summer add a few drops of vinegar before serving. In winter add a knob of butter and a little fresh ground black pepper before serving.

Sowing for Succession – CABBAGE

Variety	Sow Date	Spacing for Small Hearts	Spacing for Large Hearts	Harvest Period*
Hispi	Early February (with heat)	45 x 22cm (18 x 9in)	———	June
Spitfire	Early February (with heat)	45 x 22cm (18 x 9in)	———	July
Quickstep	Mid March	35 x 35cm (14 x 14 in)	45 x 45cm	July to September
Minicole	Mid March	35 x 35cm (14 x 14in)	45 x 45cm (18 x 18in)	August to September
Ruby Ball	Mid March	35 x 35cm	45 x 45cm	July to October
Hawke	Mid May	35 x 35cm	45 x 45cm	October to December
January King (Late Stock 3)	Late May	———	45 x 45cm	November to January
Tundra	Late May	———	50 x 50cm (20 x 20in)	December to March
Durham Early	July 25	30 x 10cm	30 x 30cm	April to May
Avoncrest	July 25	30 x 10cm (12 x 4in)	30 x 30cm (12 x 12in)	May

* Harvest period includes the standing time following maturity.

Growers' Timetable – CABBAGE

1. Spring cabbage

25 July	Sow seeds 2cm (¾in) deep in a nursery bed (sow earlier or later according to district) .
September	Transplant in rows 30cm (12in) apart with 10cm (4in) between the plants.
	Keep weed free.
Winter	Protect from pigeons and rabbits
March	Top dress with 125g per sq m (3oz per sq yd) of 10% nitrogen.
April	Keep weed free.
	Harvest to use as greens, leave every third plant to heart up.
May	Harvest hearts as required.

2. Hispi cabbage for June harvest

February	Sow seeds in a tray of compost and germinate in a heated propagator.
	As soon as the seedlings are large enough to handle, prick out into root trainers or individual 7cm (3in) pots.
	Place on the staging and grow on.
April	Harden off.
	Water with liquid fertiliser and plant out 22cm (9in) apart in rows 45cm (18in) apart. Cover with fleece.
May	Top dress with 10% nitrogen fertiliser – 125g per sq m (3oz per sq yd).
	Control weeds with a dutch hoe.
June	Harvest as soon as mature.

3. Summer cabbage

Mid-March	Sow seeds 2cm (¾in) deep in a seed bed (or raise plants in a greenhouse).
Early-May	Transplant into a firm bed 35cm x 35cm (14in x 14in).
	Water until established.
	Protect from cabbage root fly with fleece or collars – see page 48.
June	Top dress with 10% nitrogen fertiliser – 125g per sq m (3oz sq yd).
	Control weeds.
July/September	In dry weather water two weeks before harvest.
	Harvest as required. Cut cross on top of stem for second crop.

4. Winter cabbage

Late May	Sow seeds 2cm (¾in) deep in a seed bed.
Early-June	Transplant on to a firm bed 50cm x 50cm (20in x 20 in).
	Protect from cabbage root fly.
Summer	Protect from caterpillars.
	Water during very dry weather.
	Control weeds with a dutch hoe.
Winter	Harvest as required.
	Remove dead leaves.

CALABRESE

Brassica oleracea

Calabrese is also known as American, Italian or green sprouting broccoli. It is an annual plant that looks rather like cauliflower, until it produces flower buds. The flowers are the edible part, they are dark green and much more loosely packed than the cauliflower buds. Calabrese is a very quick maturing plant, producing a crop in as little as 75 days from sowing.

Soil

Calabrese is a brassica and will grow in any fertile soil with a pH between 5.5 and 7.0. It should not be grown more often than one year in three as a precaution against the disease 'clubroot'.

Sowing

Early crops are raised by germinating in a propagator, pricking out individually into pots or root trainers and grown on in a cold greenhouse or cold frame and transplanted. Later crops are best direct sown and thinned out. A fine tilth is needed to obtain an even sowing depth of 2cm (¾in).

Spacing

Plant spacing has a big effect on the spear size but very little effect on the total yield. Wider spacings give an increased yield of side shoots which develop after the central spear has been harvested.

Calabrese. This main head is ready for harvest. A second crop of side shoots will follow in two or three weeks.

one week after the final thinning.

Watering
If the soil is dry at sowing time, the bottom of the drill is soaked before sowing. Transplants, especially bare root ones, need a daily watering of 140ml (¼pt) per plant – applied directly to the base of the plant.

Established plants are given up to 22 litres per sq m (4gal per sq yd) once a week, if water is scarce, a single watering 2 to 3 weeks before harvest gives the best possible return.

Harvest
The central spear is the first to develop and is cut before the individual buds begin to separate. The head is cut off horizontally leaving a centimetre of stalk above the leaves. The sideshoots are smaller but there is more of them, these are harvested as they mature by snapping off or cutting with a sharp knife.

If harvesting is delayed the buds open into yellow flowers, these are no good to eat but they attract lots of pollinating insects into the garden.

Star Varieties
Mercedes
Quick maturing therefore good to grow for an early crop, large heads.

Green Comet
Produces sideshoots very freely after the main head has been harvested.

Corvet
The most suitable variety for Scotland and Northern England.

Cooking
Steam or boil until only just tender, calabrese needs less cooking than cauliflower.

Freezing
Blanch in boiling water for 30 seconds and drain. Cool in cold water, drain and freeze.

A spacing of 30 x 15cm (12 x 6in) gives fairly equal amounts from both central spears and side shoots. This helps to spread the crop over a longer season.

Fertilising
For maximum yields 125g per sq m (3oz per sq yd) of 10% nitrogen fertiliser is applied before planting. For direct sown crops the nitrogen is applied as a top dressing

Grower's Timetable – CALABRESE	
March	Sow an early variety in a propagator.
	Prick out into root trainers and grow on in cool greenhouse.
April	Harden off.
	Plant out in rows 30cm (12in) apart with 15cm (6in) between plants.
	Cover the plants with cloches or horticultural fleece.
May	Prepare a fine tilth and sow seeds 2cm (¾ in) deep thinly insitu in rows spaced 30cm (12in) apart.
June	Thin seedlings to 15cm (6in) Make a third and final sowing early this month.
	Harvest the early crop as it matures.
	Control weeds.
	Water as necessary.
July to	Continue to harvest, water and control weeds.
October	Cover with fleece to protect from cabbage caterpillars.

CARROT
Daucus carota
Wild carrots, with thin pale roots, occur naturally in many parts of the world. The cultivated carrot originated in Afghanistan during the twelfth century from where it spread throughout the world; carrots were first recorded in Britain during the fifteenth century. The carrot is a biennial which is grown as an annual. It is harvested halfway through its life cycle for its nutritious, orange/red tap-root. The orange colour of carrots is due to a chemical that changes into Vitamin A – it is said that this substance improves night vision.

The carrot is a fairly hardy plant but severe frost will destroy leaves and any exposed root. Sowings of three different varieties at the correct dates will provide a harvest of fresh carrots from June until January.

Soil
The soil type has a large influence upon the quality of the crop. A light, friable, well-drained soil

with lots of organic matter and a pH about neutral (7) will produce good carrots. Stony soils, or indeed any soil that does not allow easy root penetration, will produce inferior carrots with many forked roots. The common belief that carrots will not succeed in freshly manured soils has not been proved scientifically. Fresh manure may cause problems but the addition of well-rotted manure or compost is desirable.

Sowing

With the exception of small round varieties, carrots do not transplant successfully. A fine tilth is needed to obtain an even sowing depth as carrot seeds are rather small. Seeds are sown thinly at a depth of 12mm (½in).

On soil beds that contain very few weed seeds, carrots need not be sown in rows but broadcast thinly over the area. One hand weeding at the seedling stage may be necessary but once the carrots produce true leaves, weeds which germinate later will be shaded out. Carrots grown in this way produce very high yields.

Space

Close spacing results in small roots and conversely wider space results in big roots. The highest yields are obtained by sowing in rows 15cm (6in) apart. Thinning is not usually necessary for early carrots but maincrop carrots should be thinned to 5cm (2in) apart, this spacing gives medium sized carrots, larger roots can be obtained by increasing the spacing – with little effect on total yield.

Fertilising

A good crop of carrots is usually obtained from a well-managed soil without any additional fertiliser. For maximum yields 70g per sq m (2oz per sq yd) of super phosphate and 35g per sq m (1 oz per sq yd) of sulphate of potash are raked into the soil before sowing and 25g sq metre (¾oz per sq yd) of 10% nitro-

gen is applied as a top dressing 2 weeks after the first true leaves appear.

Water

Carrots must be watered with care as a lot of water can result in rapid leaf growth and little root growth. The soil should not be allowed to become too dry and in drought conditions 11 litres per sq m (2gal per sq yd) should be given every 10 to 14 days. Watering mature carrots in dry soil may cause the roots to split – either in the soil or upon harvesting.

Harvest

Carrots can be harvested as soon as they are large enough to eat. The largest roots are pulled out by hand leaving the smaller ones to grow. As the roots become larger a fork is necessary to loosen the soil, otherwise the leaves break off and the root remains in the ground. Leaves act as wicks and if left on they cause the carrots to dehydrate. It is advisable therefore to remove the leaves as part of the harvesting operation.

Succession

Three sowings will give a succession of carrots from June to January, after which time stored or frozen carrots can be used.

The first sowing is made as soon as the soil is warm enough, in most seasons this will be around the end of March using an early variety like Amsterdam Forcing, or a Nantes type. A second sowing of an early or mid season type is made in late April and the final sowing in May using a maincrop variety. The first sowings will provide carrots from July until October and the final sowing will provide carrots for winter use and storing.

Cloches or polythene sheets can be used to produce carrots a month earlier than the dates given above see page 60. An alternative method of obtaining a very early crop is to sow seeds of the Paris

Market type (eg Rondo) in modules in a greenhouse and transplant at the fourth or fifth leaf stage.

Carrot fly

In most areas some protection against carrot fly is essential. See page 48-49.

Storing

Where possible carrots are best stored in the ground (with some frost protection) and lifted as required throughout the winter. Chantenay and Autumn King are the best varieties to store as they are the most frost resistant. In early December (but not before) some additional protection is given in the form of a 15cm (6in) layer of wheat straw held in position by a net or horticultural fleece. Where mice are likely to be a nuisance a covering of soil may be used instead of straw. Slugs may also cause damage, these can be controlled by applying a sprinkling of slug pellets before covering the crop.

It is possible to store carrots in slatted wooden boxes with the roots separated by layers of sand. This method is only successful if the roots are undamaged by lifting. Leaves must be carefully twisted off as any damage to the crown results in the death and decay of

Carrot varieties

RONDO   TAMINO   ASTRA   St. VALERY   VITA LONGA

the root. Carrots stored in this way will begin to shrivel after 8 or 9 weeks.

Star Varieties

First sowing
Amsterdam Forcing
Minicor

Second sowing
Chantenay Red Cored
Royal Chantenay

Third Sowing
Autumn King
Vita Longa

Cooking

The skin on a carrot is extremely thin and peeling is therefore unnecessary. Clean the roots by lightly brushing with a vegetable brush or scraping with a sharp knife.

Carrots are delicious when steamed. Small early carrots can be cooked whole, larger roots are best when sliced obliquely (similar to runner beans) before steaming. Remove from heat when just tender, or sooner if crisp carrots are preferred.

Freezing.

To freeze, prepare as for cooking, blanch for one minute, cool and freeze. Frozen carrots lose some of their crispness.

Grower's Timetable – CARROTS	
March	Prepare a fine tilth over a fertile, deeply worked soil.
	Sow seeds thinly in rows 15cm (6in) apart. Use an early variety.
April	Repeat the early sowing using Chantenay Red-Cored, or similar.
May	Sow Autumn King, or similar thinly in rows 15cm (6in) apart.
	Control weeds.
	Protect from carrot fly (see page 48).
June	Thin Autumn King to 5cm (2in) apart. Water with care as and when necessary.
	Harvest earliest sowings by selecting largest roots.
December	Cover Autumn King with leaves or straw to protect from frost (caution MICE!)
	Or lift all remaining carrots and store or freeze.

Cauliflowers must be harvested as soon as they are ready. It takes only three days for the left hand cauliflower to become like the one on the right

CAULIFLOWER & SPROUTING BROCCOLI

Brassica oleracea

Originating in the Mediterranean, this plant was not cultivated until the late 1700s. It is a close relative of the cabbage; the main difference being the growth of a large group of flower buds with thick, fleshy stalks. These buds form a compact dome shaped head that is usually white, although there are varieties with other colours including red and light green. Most cauliflowers are annuals that are harvested in the same year as sown. Others are biennials that require a period of cold before they will form a curd. These are very useful as they provide cauliflowers in late winter and early spring.

Winter cauliflower plants are very hardy but their curds are not; this makes them unsuitable for growing in the colder areas of Britain.

Sprouting broccoli is closely related to cauliflower, unlike cauliflower however it produces flower buds in groups on the ends of sideshoots. The plants of sprouting broccoli withstand most winter conditions and produce either purple or white flower heads from March to May. This is a very useful vegetable as it crops at a time when other fresh vegetables are in short supply.

Soil

Cauliflowers need to make rapid and uninterrupted growth in order to produce the leaves that will provide the materials for curd growth. The soil must therefore be very well prepared with lots of organic matter to supply both water and nutrients. It is important that the pH is somewhere between 6.5 and 7.5. The soil needs to be firm to provide a stable anchorage; this is best achieved by preparing well in advance and leaving it to consolidate. The old practice of treading soil to obtain compaction does more harm than good.

Sowing and Planting

Seeds are sown in a greenhouse to provide transplants for early production and in a seed bed for bare root transplants of later types. It is better practice to raise all plants individually in pots or root trainers as this reduces transplanting check and gives some control over soil born pests and diseases. Seeds are sown 1.5cm (¾in) deep.

Plants are hardened off and transplanted into the final positions **well before the stems are pencil thickness.** Transplants are watered an hour before and immediately after planting.

Spacing – CAULIFLOWER

The size of the curd is directly related to the space in which the plant grows; the more space the larger the curd and visa versa. The time of year is also important, early cauliflowers are more closely spaced than later types.

Spacing for average sized curds:

Early summer planted out in March	50 x 50cm (20 x 20in)
Autumn maturing planted out in May	60 x 60cm (24 x 24in)
Winter cauliflowers planted out in June	76 x 76cm (30 x 30in)

Spacing for mini-cauliflower: ie high yields of curds 4cm to 9cm (1½in to 3½in) diameter.
(Note: not all varieties are suitable for this treatment. Kings offer Snowball and Snow Crown which are ideal).
Sow in situ with rows 23cm (9in) apart and thin to 10cm (4in) along the row.
The curds all mature at about the same time and are ideal for home freezing.

Spacing for sprouting broccoli
These plants require a lot of space but this is offset by high yields. Space plants at least 1m apart (3ft 3in).

Fertilising

Summer cauliflower must be kept growing without check, otherwise they will produce tiny immature heads (this is called 'buttoning'). Two applications of nitrogen fertiliser, along with adequate water, is a good insurance against buttoning. Maximum yields are obtained by raking in 80g per square metre (3oz per sq yd) of 10% nitrogen fertiliser before transplanting and top dressing with a similar amount 6 weeks later.

Cauliflowers planted in July for early spring production should not be given any nitrogen fertiliser. The aim is to have a sturdy plant that will withstand low temperatures. In late winter early growth is encouraged by a top dressing of 10% nitrogen fertiliser applied at the rate of 80g per square metre (3oz per sq yd)

Watering

Summer cauliflowers are very susceptible to water shortage. If watering is not practical the spacings recommended above should be increased to give each plant a greater volume of soil from which to draw water. Weed control and mulching help to conserve soil water.

Where possible, water once each week with up to 22 litres per sq m (4gal per sq yd). If water is in short supply, a single watering will have most effect if applied 2 to 3 weeks before harvest. This coincides with the time when the leaves at the centre of the plants begin a spiral twist.

Winter cauliflower and sprouting broccoli should not require any watering, apart from that necessary to establish the transplants. In exceptional seasons of low rainfall some watering may be necessary in August and September.

Harvest

Cauliflowers must be harvested as soon as they are ready otherwise they discolour and 'blow'. The curds are extremely delicate and even the slightest damage will allow the entry of bacteria and the start of decay. Harvest by cutting through the stem in such a way that several leaves are harvested with the curd and the oldest leaves are left on the stalk. Protect the curd by gently folding the leaves over the top. Cool the cauliflower as quickly as possible by placing it in a refrigerator. This maintains the cauliflower in peak condition by stopping its growth.

Sprouting broccoli is harvested when the flowerbuds are still forming a tight cluster. Break off each cluster together with the top one or two leaflets. After initial harvest buds, lower down the shoots develop producing another crop. If picked regularly the plant will yield for several weeks.

Star Varieties

Early summer
Dominant
Matures in 3 months after transplanting, good quality curds.

Summer
Candid Charm
Excellent quality, well protected heads
Dok
Deep, well-protected heads. Suitable for summer production only.

Autumn
Barrier Reef
Australian bred, large vigorous plants with excellent heads.

Winter
Inca
(mild districts only) - Matures in March, solid heads.
Walcheren Winter Armado
April and the later *Walcheren Winter Maystar* - winter hardy in most districts, white solid heads.

The variety *Romanesco* produces pointed lime green heads of excellent flavour. The yield is rather low but is well worth growing in larger gardens. Space 70 x 70cm (28 x 28in)

Sprouting broccoli

There are no distinct varieties, just early and late forms of both purple and white broccoli. Two or three plants of each type will provide a continuous supply throughout March, April and May.

Cooking

Divide cauliflower into individual florets and steam until tender. (Frozen cauliflower loses some of its crispness and is better served with a sauce.)

Sprouting broccoli is much better steamed than boiled. Add mint sauce to the purple form before serving.

Freezing

Divide the florets and drop into boiling water, leave for one minute, drain and cool quickly by dropping into cold water. Spread a single layer onto a metal dish and freeze.

Mini-cauliflower sowing and harvesting timetable

Sow	Harvest
2 April	5 July
29 April	16 July
12 May	23 July
30 May	8 August
10 June	18 August
20 June	1 September
28 June	24 September

Grower's Timetable - CAULIFLOWER

Previous autumn	Prepare cauliflower plot.
Early February	Sow seeds of Montano in a heated propagator.
March	Prick out seedlings into individual pots and grow on in greenhouse
	Sow Plana and Dok in a greenhouse or cold frame.
	Harden off Montano.
April	Transplant Montano and protect with cloches or fleece.
May	Harden off Plana and Dok.
	Sow Wallaby Transplant Plana and Dok - protect from cabbage root fly.
Late May	Sow Newton Seale (very mild areas only).
	Sow Walcheren Winter varieties Control weeds.
June	Water as required late June.
	Transplant Wallaby July.
	Protect from cabbage butterflies and moths.
	Control weeds Water as required mid.
July	Transplant Walcheren varieties.
Late July	Transplant Newton Seale (very mild areas only).
All season	Harvest as soon as ready.

Grower's Timetable - SPROUTING BROCCOLI

Late May	Sow a few seeds of early and late purple and early and late white.
Mid July	Transplant into final position.
Summer	Protect from Cabbage caterpillars. Control weeds.
November	Stake and tie.
Winter	In cold windy districts, protect from north and east winds with a fleece barrier.
March/April	Harvest twice each week.

CELERIAC

Apium graveolens var rapaceum

Celeriac is a biennial which is grown as an annual for its celery flavoured root. It is a very useful vegetable that ought to be more widely grown, especially in gardens where soil conditions and slugs make celery growing difficult. The roots can be lifted as required throughout autumn and winter. Celeriac can be shredded in salads, cubed and boiled as a vegetable or used as a celery substitute in soups and casseroles.

Bolting

Many biennials will bolt if they are subject to cold at a certain, sensitive stage of their development. Celeriac plants are at this sensitive stage when they are just large enough for hardening-off. If the weather is cold, hardening off should be delayed. The plants can be held back by clipping the tops off with scissors, down to a height of 8cm (3in) and hardened-off later.

Soil

Celeriac will grow in any fertile soil with a pH between 6.5 and 7.5.

Sowing

Seeds are sown from mid-February to mid-March in a cold frame or greenhouse, this gives Celeriac the long season it needs. Sown in trays of multipurpose compost and placed in a propagator set at 16°C. Alternatively they can be germinated in the house and moved into better light as soon as the seedlings emerge. When large enough to handle they are pricked out into 7cm (3in) pots, one plant in each pot. By this method an excellent root system is produced and there is virtually no transplanting check to growth – provid-

Growing CELERIAC

Early March	Sow seeds in a tray of multipurpose compost and germinate in a propagator.
	Prick out into individual 7cm (3in) pots.
	Grow on in a greenhouse or cold frame.
Late May	Harden off.
June:	Plant out 30cm (12in) apart in rows 40cm (16in). apart.
Summer	Control weeds. Water if needed.
September	Remove side shoots
	Draw a little soil around the bulb.
September to February	Harvest as required.

ing they are well hardened off.

Spacing

For maximum yield plants are spaced 30cm (12in) apart along rows which are 40cm (16in) apart.

Fertilising

If the soil is well supplied with organic matter additional fertiliser is unnecessary.

Watering

In very dry weather celeriac should receive 11 litres per sq m (2gal per sq yd) each week, this amount is of course reduced according to rainfall.

Blanching

During September any shoots that are growing from the side of the bulb are cut off and a little soil is drawn around the bulb to keep it white.

Harvesting

Celeriac is very hardy and can be left in the ground until required for use, in cold districts cover with leaves or straw in November. Harvest from September onwards by digging up with a fork and then trimming off leaves and fibrous roots.

Star Varieties

Balder
Round medium sized roots which are excellent cooked or raw.

Cooking

Peel and cube the root and either boil in water with the lid on or steam. Mash with a little butter and serve hot. When serving raw in salad add a little lemon juice to prevent discolouring.

Celeriac

CELERY

Apium graveolens var dulce

A native of Europe and Asia, this biennial plant is grown for its crisp leaf stalks. Celery has been in cultivation for over 2,000 years and is widely grown in the cooler parts of the world.

Celery is not easy to grow for the following reasons:

❑ The seeds are sometimes difficult to germinate.

❑ Young plants with five or more leaves will bolt if subject to temperatures below 10C (50F) for more than a week.

❑ It needs a lot of water but has a shallow rooting system.

❑ Winter varieties need earthing up; this makes slug control diffi cult.

Soil

The soil must be very water retentive, well supplied with organic matter and have a pH of not less than 6.5 (the ideal range is 6.6 to 6.8).

Sowing and Planting

Self-blanching varieties mature from August to October and are sown in late March or early April. The seed is sown in pots, left uncovered and germinated in a propagator set at 15°C (60°F). The seedlings are pricked out into individual 7cm (3in) pots and grown on in the greenhouse. In late May or early June they are gradually hardened off before being planted outside. Alternatively, plants may be purchased.

Winter celery matures from November onwards. The plants are raised in the same way but unlike the self blanching, which is grown on the flat, winter celery is planted in the bottom of a trench, 22cm (9in) deep and the width of a spade. The soil from the trench is piled neatly along either side to be used later for backfilling.

Spacing

For maximum yields, self blanching celery is grown on the square with 28cm (11in) between the plants and the same distance between the rows. If slender hearts are required they are planted 15cm (6in) apart both ways.

Trench celery is planted 30cm (12in) apart along the bottom of the trench.

Fertilising

The element sodium (present in common salt) has a beneficial effect on celery. A top dressing of nitrate of soda provides both sodium and nitrogen; this is applied at the rate of 60g per sq m (2oz per sq yd) soon after the plants have become established. Nitrate of soda absorbs water and becomes damp; it is therefore kept in a sealed container.

Watering

Watering improves both the size and the quality of celery. Regular watering is essential otherwise the sticks become stringy. Up to 11 litres per sq m (4gal per sq yd) can be applied twice a week during the height of the summer.

Blanching

It is not necessary to blanch self blanching celery, but nevertheless it is improved by tying black polythene around the stems for 2 weeks before harvest.

Blanching is necessary for winter celery. In late August the stalk area of each plant is wrapped in newspaper to prevent soil from getting in between the stalks. The plants are not buried all at once, the trench is first half filled with soil and left for 3 weeks, it is then filled to the top. Earthing up is done 3 weeks later to form a ridge that completely covers the stems, the leaves are never covered.

Harvest

Self blanching celery is less hardy than the trench types and should be harvested before November. Trench celery is improved by frost and should be ready from November onwards. Later in the winter trench celery should be given some protection otherwise hard frost will cause rotting.

Harvest both types by simply digging up and trimming off the roots.

Star Varieties

Celebrity
Self blanching and resistant to bolting.

Pascal
A trench variety with stringless sticks and a good flavour.

Cooking

Although usually eaten raw, celery makes an excellent vegetable. Either cut into 7cm (3in) sticks and steam until tender or blanch and then braise in the oven for half an hour on Reg4 350°F (180°C).

Grower's Timetable – CELERY

Autumn	Prepare the ground by mixing lots of organic matter into the soil.
Late March	Sow seeds in pots, place uncovered into a propagator.
April	Prick out into individual 7cm (3in) pots and grow on.
Late May	Harden off plants with extreme care – OR purchase plants
Early June	Plant out self blanching types on the square 28 cm (11in) apart for large heads and 15 cm (6 in) for slender heads.
	Dig a trench 22cm (9in) deep and a spade's width and plant a single row of winter celery 30cm (12in) apart.
June - September	Water regularly.
	Control weeds.
	Control slugs.
	Top dress once with 60g per sq metre (2oz per sq yd) nitrate of soda.
Late August	Begin blanching the winter crop. Harvest self blanching types as required.
October	Complete earthing up the winter crop.
November onwards	Harvest winter crop as required.

Chicory

CHICORY

Cichorium intybus
This plant grows in the wild in this country and has been used for centuries both as a cooked vegetable and as a salad. It is a hardy perennial with a large taproot. The root may be roasted, ground and used as a coffee substitute or it may be potted up and used to produce tight, blanched lettuce-like heads known as 'chicons'.

The soil

A deeply worked soil is essential for the taproot to develop fully. However, unlike root vegetables such as parsnips, it does not really matter if the root becomes divided into fangs. Almost any soil with a pH between 5.5 and 7.0 will grow chicory; better roots are obviously obtained in fertile soils than in impoverished ones.

Sowing

Chicory plants should not be raised indoors for transplanting as an early crop will run to seed. Sowing should be delayed until early June. The soil is raked to a fine tilth and seeds are sown very thinly, 2.5cm (1in) deep in drills in the open ground.

Spacing

Rows are spaced 30cm (12in) apart and individual plants are thinned to a distance of 22cm (9in) along the row.

Fertilising

A top dressing two weeks after thinning of 70g per sq m (2oz per sq yd) of 10% nitrogen fertiliser encourages the growth of leaves necessary for the formation of good roots. No more nitrogen should be applied otherwise leaf growth may be at the expense of root growth.

Watering

Watering may be necessary to aid germination. After that time chicory is left unwatered to encourage deep root growth, unless the season is very dry when a watering of 22 litres per sq m (4 gal per sq yd) is given every 2 weeks, or more often if the plants show signs of wilting.

Harvesting and Forcing

The large roots are dug as required in late autumn and early winter for the forcing of chicons. The leaves are cut off, just above the crown and the bottom of the roots trimmed to leave around 30 cm (12 in) of the thickest parts.

The roots are planted up in deep pots or boxes in moist sandy soil or moist peat with the crowns just protruding above the surface. The roots can be packed fairly tightly with just 7cm (3in) in between. Some varieties require a covering of peat to a depth of 15cm (6in), whilst other varieties will form tight chicons without; all varieties must be forced in complete darkness, otherwise the chicons will be green and bitter.

The temperature for forcing should be over 10°C (50°F). In four weeks or so the chicons should be fully formed and about 17cm (7in) tall. Chicons are harvested by breaking off with care; breaking off rather than cutting encourages a second (but smaller) crop to grow. It is better to harvest chicons as near to the time of use as possible as they wilt very quickly.

In November, after the tops have died back any unused roots should be lifted and trimmed. They will store if packed in dry sand and kept cool. The roots are taken from the store for forcing as required.

Star Variety

Zoom
The white chicons remain compact without a covering of peat.

Grower's Timetable – CHICORY

Early June	Select a site that has been deeply worked and manured in the previous autumn. Rake to a fine tilth and sow seeds as thinly as possible 2.5cm (1in) deep in rows 30cm (12in) apart.
July	Thin the seedlings to a distance of 22cm (9in) along the row.
July to October	Water if necessary. Keep weed free.
October onwards	Lift the roots as required and use them for forcing chicons.
November	Lift remaining roots and store.

CHINESE CABBAGE

Brassica rapa

A biennial plant which is grown as a short-lived annual, Chinese cabbage looks like a very large and pale cos lettuce. Given the right conditions it is a quick maturing crop, easy to grow and will not bolt. Chinese cabbage can be grown after early potatoes or in ground that would otherwise be idle during the latter part of the season. This vegetable is very susceptible to all the pests and diseases which are likely to affect cabbages.

Soil

Almost any soil that is not too sandy and holds lots of moisture is suitable, the pH is not critical and chinese cabbage will grow at any level between 5.0 and 7.0. Chinese cabbage must be grown in good light as it will not tolerate shade. On open sites some protection from the wind is desirable.

Sowing and Planting

If sown too early Chinese cabbage will bolt, the sowing date needs to be after the 1st of July and before the end of August. Seeds are sown in a fine tilth 1cm (½in) deep. If plants are raised in a greenhouse they need to be in individual pots to allow for transplanting without any root disturbance.

Spacing

Rows need to be 40cm (16in) apart with plants spaced the same distance along the row.

Fertilising

Chinese cabbage is a leaf vegetable which grows very quickly – its nitrogen requirement is therefore very high. An application of 100g per sq m (4oz per sq yd) of 10% nitrogen fertiliser is applied as a top dressing soon after the plants have passed the six leaf stage.

Watering

The soil must be kept moist at all times as any check to growth encourages bolting. Water is applied directly to the soil without wetting the plants at a rate of 11 litres per sq m (2gal sq yd) each week. A mulch is also applied to prevent the soil surface from drying out.

Tying

Some varieties form a more compact heart when tied with raffia, a single tie about two thirds the way up is sufficient.

Harvest

Chinese cabbage very soon run to seed and should be harvested as soon as they are ready. Harvest by cutting off just above ground level. The stump will regrow and produce a crop of edible leaves.

Star Variety

Tip Top
Matures in 60 days, heavy heads with some resistance to bolting.

Cooking

Chinese cabbage is usually eaten

raw in a similar way to lettuce. If cooked they should be stir fried in the Chinese fashion.

Pak-choi
This is a type of Chinese cabbage which does not form a head. It is grown for the thick, fleshy leaf stalks and the large spoon shaped leaves. These are harvested when young and cooked before serving.

Pak-choi is grown in the same way as described for Chinese cabbage except that it is better to start the seeds in a greenhouse, harden off and plant out when the air temperature is above 10°C (50°F).

Grower's Timetable – CHINESE CABBAGE	
May	Sow seeds of the pak-choi type in pots in a greenhouse.
June	Harden off and plant outside, spacing plants 40cm (16 in) each way.
July	Sow seeds of hearting Chinese cabbage in rows 1cm (½in) deep.
August	Thin seedlings to 40cm (16in). Control weeds. Top dress with 100g per sq m (4oz per sq yd) of 10% nitrogen fertiliser.
	Water in dry weather and mulch well.
	Harvest pak-choi.
September	Tie hearted types with raffia.
	Harvest as soon as ready.

COURGETTES AND MARROWS
Cucurbita pepo.

This annual plant originated in Mexico and is now widely grown throughout the world. The cylindrical fruits are harvested as courgettes when small and marrows when large. The large leaves and soft stems are damaged by hail and killed by frost.

Soil
Marrows need a free draining soil and a constant supply of water; the best way of meeting these two demands is to form a mound by mixing large quantities of organic matter into a square metre (square yard) of soil. Any pH between 5.5 and 7.0 is suitable.

Custard white

A courgette and three days later

Sowing and Planting
Early crops are grown by raising plants in a greenhouse or cold frame. In mid to late April seeds are sown individually in 12cm (5in) pots, containing multi-purpose compost. Each seed is held between finger and thumb and pushed into the compost to a depth of 3cm (1in). A minimum compost temperature of 13°C (56°F) is required for germination, this is achieved by placing the pots in a propagator or leaving them in the

house. After germination they are kept in a cold greenhouse or cold frame, some additional frost protection may be required. The plants are hardened off at the end of May and planted out in early June. The pot which contained the plant is sunk alongside, its rim at soil level. The plant is watered by filling the pot, this directs water to the root and prevents soil erosion.

A marrow bed provides ideal conditions for slugs; where these are a problem chemical or beer traps are sited at planting time.

Spacing
Marrows and courgettes are planted 1m (1yd) apart. Trailing marrows are much larger than bush types, if trained up a net or trellis they need only the same ground space. If trailing marrows are allowed to trail across the ground, provision must be made to allow for stems up to two metres (2yds) long.

Watering
Marrows and courgettes require a lot of water, especially when flowering and in dry weather may need watering twice a week. The pot alongside the plant is filled as many times as is necessary to keep the soil moist. A mulch of compost

over the soil will help to conserve water.

Pollination
Plants carry separate male and female flowers; the male contains anthers which produce pollen whilst the female has stigmas to receive the pollen. The easiest way to tell which is which is to look at the flower stalk, the male stalk is plain whilst there is a small fruit on the stalk of the female flower. Daylength influences the type of flowers which are produced, early in the season there are more male than female flowers whilst the reverse is true as the days lengthen.

If the female flowers are not pollinated the marrows will not form. Bumble bees usually, but not always, pollinate marrows. Hand pollination is easy, the male flower is removed and stripped of its petals. The anthers are then brought in contact with the stigmas of the female flower, one male may be used to pollinate several flowers or it may be left inside a single female flower.

Harvest
Courgettes: Remove the courgette as soon as it is large enough by cutting through the stalk with a sharp knife. *Caution:* The fruits

grow very quickly and if harvesting is delayed for more than a day the courgette becomes a marrow. Regular harvesting increases the numbers of courgettes, the plant in the photograph on page 40 produced over fifty fruits whilst a similar plant produced just seven marrows.

Marrows: Marrows for immediate use can be harvested at any stage of their growth by cutting through the stalk with a sharp knife. Marrows required for storing must be left on the plant to ripen. A ripe marrow gives a hollow sound when tapped with the knuckles whilst the sound from an unripe one is much duller.

Storing
Ripe marrows will keep for 2 or 3 months. Ideally undamaged fruits are hung in a net in an airy, cool but frost free building.

Star Varieties
Bush for courgette production:

Ambassador
A heavy cropper, courgettes are dark green with a smooth glossy skin.

Bush for marrow production:
Minipak
Attractive green and white striped fruits, early and prolific.

Trailing for marrow production:
Long Green Trailing
Large marrows with pale and dark green stripes.

Cooking
Courgettes. Wipe the fruit and slice into rings 1cm (½in) thick. Fry in a little butter or oil, sprinkle on a little black pepper and serve.

Marrows. Wash but do not peel. Cut lengthways through the middle and scoup out the seeds. Cut into chunks, place in a greased tin and bake in a hot oven until tender.

Grower's Timetable – COURGETTES AND MARROWS

April	Sow seeds individually in 12cm (5in) pots of multi-purpose compost and germinate at 13C (56F)
	Prepare a bed by mixing large quantities of organic matter with the soil to produce a raised mound.
	If growing trailing marrows, fix a net or trellis to support the runners.
May	Harden off the plants at the end of the month.
June	Plant out on top of the mound 1m (1yd) apart. Sink the empty pot flush with the surface, as near to the plant as possible.
	Take precautions against slugs. Train the first shoots onto the support.
July	For marrow production pollinate the first female flowers with pollen from a male flower
	Harvest courgettes as soon as they are large enough.
	Protect developing marrows from the soil by placing a small board under each one.
Aug/Sept	Continue to harvest both courgettes and marrows until cold weather stops production

---

LAND CRESS
Barbarea verna also known as Land Cress and American Cress

The cress in which just the seed leaves are eaten is best grown inside from rape, mustard or cress seeds. When this type of cress is grown outside the small leaves become contaminated with soil and are very difficult to wash. The species in the title is quite different, it is very similar to water cress in both looks and taste. Land cress is a hardy biennial which is grown as an annual. This salad is strongly recommended as it is easy to grow, yields well and has an excellent taste.

Soil
Any moist fertile soil will support land cress. The site needs to be in full sun for the best results.

Sowing
This crop can be sown in early spring as soon as the soil becomes workable. The soil is raked to a fine tilth and seeds are sown thinly in drills 1cm (½in) deep.

Spacing
Rows are spaced 15cm (6in) apart and plants are thinned along the row to 10cm (4in) apart.

Fertilising
This crop is harvested early in its growing period and no additional fertiliser is necessary in a fertile soil.

Watering
For summer sowings the soil should be wetted to a depth of 30cm (1ft) before sowing, spring sowings are unlikely to require watering.

Land cress

Harvest
Land cress is very hardy and can be harvested throughout the year. Whole plants can be taken or individual leaves picked as required.

As the plants become older the taste gets stronger, if a supply of milder tasting leaves is needed then three sowings should be made during the season.

Grower's Timetable – LAND CRESS	
April	Sow seeds 1cm (½in) deep in rows 15cm (6in) apart.
May	Thin seedlings to 10cm (4in) apart. Control weeds.
June	Make a second sowing. Harvest as required.
July	Make the third sowing.
onwards	Control weeds. Harvest as required. Dig up and discard before the following spring.

Ridge cucumber

Crystal Apple cucumber

CUCUMBER, RIDGE
Cucurbitaceae sativus and Gherkins
Cucumbers have been developed from a Himalayan plant which is now very rare in the wild. It is a vigorous tender climber which is very susceptible to frost. Cucumber fruits are eaten before they ripen. Greenhouse cucumbers require protection throughout but ridge cucumbers are more hardy and just as tasty. The skin on some types of ridge cucumber is difficult to digest and these are best peeled before use. Few places in the U.K. have a climate that is mild enough for ridge cucumbers to be grown entirely outside, they can however be grown by raising the plants indoors and transplanting outside when all danger of frost is past. Ridge cucumbers can be successfully grown in a cold frame.

Soil
Although cucumbers are shallow rooted they are highly susceptible to water logging, they also require a water retentive soil with lots of organic matter. These conditions are met by mixing enough manure or compost with the soil to form a mound. The plants are then grown on the mound. A pH between 5.5 and 7 is suitable.

Sowing
Many gardeners grow cucumbers from plants purchased in late May and early June, however cucumber plants are easily raised by use of a propagator in a greenhouse (or conservatory). The following method is very successful:

1. Use clean 15cm (6 inch) pots and two thirds fill with a sterilised, free draining seed compost.

2. Hold one seed between finger and thumb and push it into the centre of the pot to a depth of one centimetre (½in).

3. Water the pots and place them in a propagator set at 25°C (75°F) or the highest setting if it is lower than this.

4. After germination, which takes about three days, leave the plants in the propagator, make sure that there is some ventilation and the propagator top is as clean as possible to admit maximum light.

5. When the seedling reaches the top of the pot, add extra compost up to within 1cm (½in) of the seed leaves.

6. Feed the plants each week with half strength tomato fertiliser.

7. When daytime temperatures are above 21°C (70°F), remove the plants from the propagator and place them in the lightest part of the greenhouse. At night cover them with a piece of horticultural fleece.

8. Transfer the plants to a cold frame and gradually harden them off by progressively removing the top.

Planting
Cucumber plants are very sensitive to cold and are carefully hardened off, this is especially true of purchased plants that may have had a chill during moving. (Plants standing on pavements outside shop doors are unlikely to survive.)

A pot size hole is dug with a trowel and water is poured in to thoroughly wet the soil. The plant is removed from its pot and placed in the hole, soil is drawn around the stem and gently firmed. A second similar hole is dug alongside the plant and the pot inserted, watering is done by filling the pot, this gets water to the roots without disturbing the soil.

Spacing
Plants are spaced 60cm (2ft) apart, after four or five true leaves have grown on each plant the top is nipped out. The sideshoots are allowed to grow and run over the soil surface.

Watering
Cucumbers and gherkins will not tolerate drought, the soil around the roots of the young plants is kept moist by watering regularly into the empty pots alongside. This level of watering is main

tained throughout flowering and fruiting.

Support
Plants are sometimes left to trail along the ground and this method is quite successful. An alternative method is to erect a trellis or vertical net, the young shoots are tied on, or threaded through after which they are left to climb.

Harvest
Ridge cucumbers and gherkins are harvested before they ripen, cucumbers are harvested when about 23cm (9in) long and gher-kins when they are 12cm (5in) long. Regular picking encourages more fruit to form and very large crops are obtained. Leaving fruits on to ripen stops the plants from producing.

Storing
Cucumbers quickly deteriorate and lose their flavour if kept in a refrigerator for more than a couple of days. They keep in good condition for up to two weeks if partially wrapped in clingfilm and stored in a cool room. Gherkins are pickled and keep indefinitely.

Star Variety
Crystal Apple
Rounded shape, high yields, excellent flavour .

Bedfordshire Prize
Early with small dark green fruits.

Gherkin
Quick growing, masses of small prickly fruits for pickling.

Cooking
Cucumbers are usually sliced and eaten raw - or made into a cold soup.

Crystal Apple cucumber from flower to ripe fruit. The label shows the best time for harvest

Grower's Timetable – CUCUMBER	
Spring	Prepare mounds by mixing large quantities of manure with soil.
Early May	Sow seeds in a heated propagator.
Mid June	Harden off or purchase plants Plant 60cm (2ft) apart, sink empty pot next to plant. Water well. If staking, erect a vertical net 120cm (4ft) high. Pinch out top of plants after 5 true leaves.
July	Thread young shoots through net or trellis.
July to September	Harvest regularly as soon as fruits are large enough. Keep well watered.

ENDIVE
Cichorium endivia
Endive is an annual which is grown for its leaves; these may be braised but are most often eaten raw in salads. Endive is an easy crop to grow and is most useful during late autumn and early winter as a lettuce substitute.

Soil
Any soil that is well supplied with organic matter will support a crop of endive. The soil from which early potatoes have been recently lifted is ideal.

Sowing
Extra care is needed if endive is to be transplanted successfully, it is therefore most often grown from seeds sown in situ. The soil is raked to a fine tilth and seeds are sown in drills 2cm (¾in) deep. Sow from late June to early August.

Spacing
Rows are spaced 30cm (12in) apart and the plants are thinned to a similar distance.

Fertilising
Fertiliser is unnecessary in a fertile soil; a single watering with a foliar feed will however increase the yield. This should be applied 3 to 4 weeks after thinning when the leaves are large enough to take up the nutrients.Phostrogen, Miracle-gro or any other well-known brand would be suitable.

Watering
Endive must be well supplied with water. 11 litres per sq m (2gal per sq yd) should be applied each week during dry weather.

Blanching
Unblanched endive is bitter and unpalatable, blanching is therefore essential. Three weeks before harvest the centre is covered with a 15cm (6in) plant pot, the holes of which have been covered with electricians' tape. In windy areas the pot is secured with two pegs and a length of string. The plants must be dry when covered otherwise the edges of the leaves may rot. Alternatively the whole plant can be tied with string in such a way that the outside leaves exclude light from the inner leaves.

Harvest
Blanched leaves are a light cream colour, these are picked as required. Alternatively the whole plant is cut off at ground level and the outer green leaves discarded.

Star Varieties
Riccia Pancallieri
Curly toothed leaves and a prostrate habit.

Jeti
Upright foliage, almost self-blanching, a single tie of string near to the top is all that is required.

Blanching endive with plant pots

Blanching endive by tying with string

Grower's Timetable – ENDIVE	
Late June –	Sow seeds 2cm (¾in) deep in rows 30cm (12in) apart.
Early August	Control weeds.
July/August	Keep the soil moist.
	Thin seedlings to 30cm (12in) apart.
September – October	Blanch as required by covering with pots or tying up.
November – December	Protect late crops with cloches.

Endive

FENNEL, FLORENCE
Foeniculum vulgare var dulce

There are two types of fennel, the feathery herb which is used for garnish and the type that forms an edible bulb – Florence fennel. Florence fennel is a half hardy annual,

Florence fennel

its bulb tastes of aniseed. It is eaten raw in salads or cooked as a vegetable. Fennel is an excellent vegetable to serve with fish.

Soil
Fennel has a high demand for water; most moisture retentive soils with a pH between 6.0 and 7.0 are suitable for this crop. Wherever possible fennel should be grown in full sun.

Sowing and Planting
The earliest crops are grown from plants raised in the greenhouse. A bolt resisting variety is selected and the seeds are sown individually in divided trays early in April. To avoid bolting the young plants are carefully hardened off during the second half of May. This early sowing produces bulbs by the end of June.

Later sowings are made in the open ground at intervals of 3 weeks. The seeds are thinly sown in drills 1cm (½in) deep.

Spacing
Rows 30cm (12in) apart with the plants 30cm (12in) apart along the row will give the largest yield.

Fertilising
Additional fertiliser is unnecessary in a well-manured soil.

Watering
Florence fennel must not be allowed to dry out otherwise it will run to seed before forming a bulb. During dry weather a weekly watering of 11 litres per sq m (2gal per sq yd) should be given. Water applied to the soil at the base of the plants is more effective than the same amount sprayed over the foliage.

Harvest
Bulbs are harvested when they are about the size of a tennis ball, by cutting off at ground level and trimming off the leaves.

Star Variety
Cantino
Resistant to bolting, has a fine aniseed flavour.

Cooking
Trim the leaves from the bulb and wash well. Cook gently in boiling salted water for 12 to 15 minutes. Take care not to overcook. Alternatively fennel may be cooked in a microwave oven.

Growers' Timetable – FLORENCE FENNEL	
Early April	Sow seeds individually in divided trays, germinate in a propagator and grow on in a greenhouse or cold frame.
Late May	Harden off the tray grown plants
Early June	Rake the fennel bed to a fine tilth.
	Sow seeds 1cm (½in) deep in rows 30cm (12in) apart.
	Plant out hardened off plants in rows 30cm (12in) apart with the plants spaced 30cm (12in) apart along the row.
	Water as necessary.
	Keep weed free.
Late June	Make a third sowing.
	Thin the earlier sowing to leave **single** plants 30cm (12in) apart.
July to September	Keep weed free.
	Thin the later sowings to leave **single** plants 30cm (12in) apart.
	Harvest as required.

FRENCH BEANS
Phaseolus vulgaris

Also called Dwarf bean, Haricot bean and Kidney bean. This plant has several names. The fresh vegetable is called 'French' and 'Dwarf' and is eaten complete with the pod whilst the ripe seeds are called 'Haricot' or 'Kidney'. In some areas of the country runner beans are also called kidney beans, these are in fact a different species.

French beans have been grown in Britain since being introduced from Mexico during the sixteenth century. The plant is a quick maturing half hardy annual with two forms, bush and climbing. The bush varieties mature more quickly than the climbing types which produce a larger crop.

Soil

French beans originated in the tropics and require a wet and warm soil. Sandy soils warm most quickly whilst clay soils hold most water; a good loam is ideal as it is half way between these two extremes. Sandy soils can be irrigated whilst clay soils can be warmed with plastic – or sowing can be delayed whilst the soil warms up. Whatever the soil type the pH needs to be between 5.5 and 6.5.

Sowing and Planting

French bean seeds should not be sown until the soil temperature is at least 10°C (50°F), even at this temperature germination is very slow and the seeds may rot in the soil. The soil is raked to a medium tilth and the seeds are sown 4 to 5cm (1 to 2in) deep. The seeds are large enough to be sown individually, the usual method is to place two seeds at each station and remove the weaker plant if both germinate.

French beans transplant well, especially if grown in root trainers or individual pots, the earliest crops are from greenhouse raised plants which must be correctly hardened off. Pot raised plants should not be planted out until the soil temperature is well over 10°C (50°F) and preferably 15°C (60°F). The foliage of french beans is damaged by the slightest frost, planting out must be delayed until all chance of frost has passed.

Spacing

When French beans are grown on the flat, paths between the rows need to be 45cm (18in) wide to allow access for picking. The highest yields are obtained by sowing double rows 15cm (6in) wide in between the paths. The best spacing along the row is 8cm (3in) from plant to plant. The plants in the double row should be staggered to give each as much space as possible.

No access is needed to plants grown on raised beds as picking is done from the paths. On these beds the best yields are obtained by spacing the rows 15cm (6in) apart with plants 8cm (3in) apart.

Climbing varieties should be given just enough space between the rows to provide access, and planted 10cm (4in) apart along the rows.

Fertilising

French beans have a high phosphate requirement, soils managed as recommended in chapter 1 should contain sufficient to meet this demand. However a good insurance policy is to sprinkle a thin band of superphosphate in a trench 5cm (2in) to the side and 5cm (2in) below the seeds just before sowing. With transplanted crops a pinch of superphosphate in each planting hole will suffice.

A top dressing of 100g per sq m (3oz per sq yd) of 10% nitrogen applied when the plants have two true leaves will boost yield. For transplanted crops the nitrogen is raked into the plant bed before planting.

Watering

Too much water during the early stages of growth results in the over-production of leaves at the expense of pods. Water is very beneficial when the crop begins to flower as it increases pod production. Frequent watering not only increases the yield, it improves the quality and delays the onset of stringiness in the pods.

During times of no rainfall 22 litres per sq m (4 gal per sq yd) should be given each week. The frequency of watering, rather than the amount, is reduced according to rainfall.

Support

Dwarf varieties are not supported Climbing varieties can be supported on canes in a similar way to runner beans. A plastic garden net with 10cm (4in) square holes, stretched between two veritcal posts is a better way as it allows for closer planting and therefore a larger yield.

Harvest

Beans must be picked when the pods have reached their maximum length but before the seeds begin to swell. Regular picking is important as this encourages the production of more flowers. Harvesting requires two hands, one to support the plant whilst the other pulls off the mature beans.

Star Varieties

Bush types:
Tendergreen
Pencil shaped, stringless pods, suitable for cooking whole.

Masterpiece
Flat podded, very heavy cropping, suitable for slicing.

Climbing types:
Hunter
Flat pods which yield a very heavy crop.
Corona D'Oro
Pencil shaped, golden yellow, stringless pods.

Cooking

Cook pencil podded varieties whole. The flat podded varieties

French beans

may be sliced in a similar way to runner beans. French beans are better boiled than steamed. Top and tail the beans. Be as economical as possible otherwise they will open during cooking. Cook in boiling, salted water until just tender. Take care not to overcook or the flavour and texture will be lost.

Freezing
French beans freeze well – especially the pencil podded varieties. Blanch in boiling water for one minute. Drain and cool in cold water. Drain again, dab dry and spread on a metal tray to freeze.

Grower's Timetable – FRENCH BEANS	
Mid May	When the soil is warm enough (over 10°C/50°F) sow seeds 4 to 5 cm (1 to 2in) deep in pairs 8cm (3in) apart along double rows which are 15cm (6in) apart.
June	Remove the weakest seedling from each pair. Control weeds.
July	Top dressing with 100g per sq m (3 oz per sq yd) of 10% nitrogen. When the first flowers open begin to water as necessary. Give each sq m (sq yd) 22l (4gal) in weeks when there is little or no rain.
August/ September	Continue to water and to control weeds. If water is in short supply, give one good watering and then mulch with compost or other suitable material. This will also control weeds. Harvest at least twice each week, take all the crop which is ready each time.

Garlic

GARLIC
Allium sativum
Originating in Central Asia, this plant has been cultivated for over 4,000 years. It is a hardy perennial, grown for the aromatic oils in its bulbs. Unlike other culinary bulbs it does not have a uniform cross section, but consists of a number of offsets (cloves) which are clumped onto a single stem. Garlic is principally used for flavouring but the leaves may be chopped and eaten in salad. In addition the oils in garlic are believed to have beneficial medicinal effects.

Soil
Garlic grows well in most soils but, in common with most other vegetables, a light, free draining, moisture retentive soil is preferred. It is most important that the site is in full sunshine, planting in shade must be avoided as garlic has only a small area of leaf to catch the light.

Planting
Before a garlic clove will form a bulb it must have a period of cold, the most convenient way of ensuring that it does, is to plant in late autumn or very early spring. A bulb is broken up into its constituent cloves – usually a dozen or more. The cloves are then planted upright with the tips just below the surface. Garlic for planting should only be purchased once as home saved bulbs will provide cloves for planting the following years.

Spacing
Rows 30cm (1ft) apart with the cloves 15cm (6in) apart along the row provides enough space for maximum yield. Good weed control (preferably by hand) is essential for this crop as the effectiveness of correct spacing is reduced by weed growth.

Fertilising
On well-managed soil additional fertiliser is unnecessary for garlic and may even be harmful.

Watering
Garlic grows early in the season

Grower's Timetable – GARLIC	
November or February	Break up a bulb of garlic into its individual cloves and select the largest. Plant cloves, with the tips just under the soil surface, 15cm (6in) apart along rows 30cm (12in) apart.
March to June	Keep weed free by hand or shallow hoeing.
July	Lift with a fork, dry thoroughly, tie into ropes and store.

when moisture levels are generally high and it is extremely unlikely that this crop would benefit from additional water. In an exceptionally dry spring on very dry soil 70ml (⅛pt) per plant per day may be given until the plants are established.

Harvest

The bulbs become dormant in the summer months and the foliage dies down. After the foliage has died down the bulbs are dug up with a fork – pulling up causes damage! The bulbs are then thoroughly dried in sun (or in an airy shed if the weather is wet).

Storing

Dry bulbs are tied in ropes to allow air circulation all around each bulb. The ropes are hung in an airy shed and bulbs are removed as required.

Star Varieties

Silverskin
Good keeper with a strong flavour.

Fructidor
Large bulbs, milder flavour.

Cooking

Garlic is used almost exclusively as a flavouring. The cloves are chopped up or squeezed through a garlic press before adding to the recipe.

Garlic growing by roses as a protection against aphids

HERBS

The two most commonly used herbs in the British kitchen are probably mint and parsley; these are therefore dealt with separately on pages 96 and 100.

Some of the other culinary herbs are hardy shrubs and are most attractive when placed in the flower garden these include, rosemary (Rosmarinus officInalis), sage (Salvia officinalis), thyme (Thymus vulgaris) which makes an excellent edging plant and bay (Laurus nobilis). Note: Bay is only hardy if left to develop naturally, bay trees which are trained as standards require winter protection. The herbaceous perennial fennel (Foeniculum vulgare) is also a suitable subject for a mixed flower border and the bronze form of this plant is particularly decorative.

Herbs suitable for growing in the vegetable garden:

BASIL

(Ocimum basilicum)
Basil is best treated as a half hardy annual. It is sown in pots in spring in a cool greenhouse, hardened off and planted out in the garden in mid June. The plants will then provide leaves until the first frosts of autumn.

Basil leaves have a strong and distinctive flavour; they are used in salads, casseroles and sauces.

CHIVE

(Allium schoenoprasum)
Chive is a hardy, herbaceous perennial which is easily grown from seeds, there is no harvest during the first year. Once established a clump of chive will produce leaves early in the year and continue to do so for several years. The clump can be propagated by lifting in spring or autumn, divided into sections and replanting. Chive flowers in mid summer and seeds freely. The leaves have a mild onion flavour and are used in salads, for flavouring sauces and as a garnish.

Garlic chives is a variety which is well worth growing. It is similar to chive in many ways but the leaves are flat and it has a mild garlic taste.

DILL

(Peucedarium graveolens)
Dill is an annual plant and several sowings are made from April until June in order to get a continuity of supply. Seeds are sown thinly and shallowly in rows 30cm (12in) apart. It grows quickly with the first harvest only 2 months from sowing. Dill requires full sun and will tolerate any soil that does not dry out in summer. Dill has feathery foliage which is used in salads and fish dishes; the seeds have a strong flavour and are used in pickles.

SORREL

(Rumex acetosa)
This perennial herb is closely related to the weed we know as dock.

A slightly acid soil is preferred and it is one of the few herbs that will tolerate some shade. Sorrel can be grown by dividing the roots of an established plant. It is also easy to grow from seed – April being the best sowing time. Sorrel produces leaves from early spring until late autumn. The flowering shoots are cut off as they appear in order to stimulate leaf growth. The leaves are cut into strips for use in salads.

TARRAGON

(Artemisia dracunculus)
There are two types of tarragon, Russian tarragon which is grown from seed and French tarragon which can only be grown from cuttings or underground runners. The French tarragon is by far the better flavoured of the two.

Tarragon is an almost hardy perennial which requires full sun and a free draining soil. The plants are spaced 60cm (24in) and should be transplanted to fresh ground every 5 or 6 years.

The leaves, which have a strong and distinctive flavour, are used for vinegar and also in chicken, fish and potato recipes.

Garlic chive

Kale stands throughout the winter in this condition

KALE

Brassica oleracea and Brassica napus (also known as Borecole)

Kale is one of the hardiest vegetables, it withstands temperatures as low as -15℃ (5˚F). It is related to cabbage, but does not form a heart. The leaves and young shoots are harvested in winter and early spring when other types of fresh vegetables may be in short supply. There are two main groups of kale; one group is grown in a similar way to cabbage and has very curled leaves, the other group (the rape kales) have plain leaves and are sown in situ as they do not withstand transplanting.

Soil

Kale will succeed in much poorer soils than cabbage, better soils however produce larger crops. A pH between 6.5 and 7.0 is ideal. The soil must be firm otherwise the plants will blow over in winter.

Sowing and Planting

Transplants are raised in a seed bed, the soil is raked to a fine tilth and seeds are sown very thinly 2cm (1in) deep. The seed bed must be kept weed free. When the plants reach a height of 10cm (4in), but before the stems are the thickness of a pencil, they are lifted and planted very firmly into their final positions.

Early spring greens can be produced by sowing under cloches in late winter.

Rape kale does not transplant; it is sown thinly in rows, the final spacing being obtained by thinning out.

Spacing

Spacing for kale depends upon the variety grown. The small varieties require 45cm(18in) each way whilst the larger varieties require 75 cm (30 in) each way.

For early spring greens sow thinly in rows 10cm (4in) apart and thin to 10cm (4in) between the plants. These are harvested when 15cm (6in) high. If the stems are left in the ground a second crop will sprout.

Fertilising

A top dressing of dried blood at the rate of 60g per sq m (2oz per sq yd) in late winter encourages the growth of young shoots. Fertiliser should not be applied in the autumn as this encourages soft, tender growth that is susceptible to frost.

Watering

If transplants are thoroughly watered in further watering is unnecessary.

Harvest

Harvest by taking the youngest leaves and sideshoots. The older leaves are left to encourage further leaf growth.

Star Varieties

Fribor
Small very hardy plants which mature from November to February.

Pentland Brig
A rape kale which matures in March and April.

Cooking

Remove the leaf stalks and wash well. Cut across the leaves to form strips 2cm (1in) wide. Cook in boiling salted, water until tender.

Grower's Timetable – KALE	
May	Sow curly kale in a seed bed.
June	Transplant into rows 45cm (18in) apart and allow 45cm (18in) between the plants. Water in. Control weeds.
July	Sow rape kale thinly in rows 45cm (18in) apart. Firm the curly kale plants by treading around the bottom of the stems.
August	Thin rape kale to a distance of 45cm (18in). Control weeds.
November - February	Harvest curly kale as needed.
March	Apply a top dressing of dried blood at the rate of 60g per sq m (2oz per sq yd) around the rape kale plants.
April	Harvest the young leaves and side shoots of rape kale.

KOHLRABI

Brassica oleracea

Kohlrabi is a biennial which is grown as an annual. A close relative of cabbage it is grown for the white flesh inside its swollen stem, this has a taste similar to the inside of a cabbage stalk and is used in the same way as a turnip, ie in casseroles or boiled as a vegetable. Kohlrabi withstands higher temperatures than turnip and is very useful during the summer as a turnip substitute. It is popular on mainland Europe and deserves to be grown more widely in this country. Garden visitors find kohlrabi to be a very interesting crop.

Soil

Although light soils are best for this crop it yields quite well on heavier soils. It will tolerate any pH between 5.5 and 7.0 although the higher pH is more suitable as it reduces the risk of clubroot disease.

Sowing and planting

A week of cold weather in spring will cause kohlrabi to bolt, outside sowing should therefore be delayed until the soil temperature is 10°C (50°F). The soil is raked to a fine tilth and drills are drawn 2cm (1in) deep; seeds are sprinkled thinly along the rows and covered by backfilling. For earlier crops plants are raised in a greenhouse, preferably in root trainers, and transplanted.

Spacing

Highest yields are obtained by spacing rows 30cm (12in) apart and thinning seedlings to 20cm (8in) apart.

Fertilising

Once seedlings are growing away a top dressing of 50g per sq m (2oz per sq yd) of 10% nitrogen fertiliser will boost yield. For transplanted crops the fertiliser is applied into the plant bed before planting.

Watering

Kohlrabi have extensive root systems and draw water from a large volume of soil; it therefore withstands dry conditions better than most brassicas. Watering can be delayed until the plants show signs of wilting; the soil should then be thoroughly wetted with 15 litres per sq m (3gal per sq yd).

Harvest

Kohlrabi is harvested by digging up with a garden fork; the root and leaves are then trimmed off. Stems up to twice the size of a tennis ball are suitable, larger than this and they become fibrous and less edible. Kohlrabi does not store well; it is better to use swedes during the winter.

Star Variety

Different varieties have different skin colours but all varieties have white flesh. Varieties with purple skins are later maturing than those with green and white skins.

White Danube

Can be allowed to grow larger than other varieties, has a juicy, crisp white flesh.

Cooking

Peel off the outer skin. Dice the flesh into 2cm (1in) cubes and boil until tender. Drain and add a knob of butter, mash with a potato masher and serve. Diced kohlrabi and diced carrots mixed makes an attractive and tasty serving.

Kohlrabi cubes are an excellent addition to stews and casseroles.

Kohlrabi compared with a size 1 hens egg

Grower'sTimetable – KOHLRABI	
March	Sow seeds inside in root trainers.
May	At the end of this month, harden off and plant outside in rows 30cm (12in) apart, allow 20cm (8in) between the plants.
	Sow seeds in drills 2cm (¾in) deep and 30cm (12in).
	Control weeds.
June	Thin seedlings to 15cm (6in) apart. Topdress with 50g per sq m (2oz per sq yd) of 10% nitrogen fertiliser.
	Make a second outside sowing.
	Harvest as soon as the stems are large enough.
	Control weeds.
July	Make a final sowing early in the month.
	Thin, fertilise, control weeds and harvest until the end of the season.

LEEK
Allium porrum

The leek is closely related to the onion but forms a cylindrical, rather than a global bulb which is blanched by excluding the light. A biennial plant that produces its elongated cylindrical bulb in the first season and a flower in the next. The leek is very winter hardy and can be harvested over a long period. It is useful for flavouring soups, stews and casseroles and can also be served as a vegetable in its own right.

Leeks are either direct sown or grown from transplants, raised in a greenhouse or seed bed. They can also be grown from 'pips'. Pips are tiny leeks that appear instead of seeds if the flower buds are shaved off just before they open.

Soil

Although most soils will produce some sort of crop, a deeply worked soil, rich in organic matter is necessary to produce really good leeks. The pH needs to be between 6.5 and 7.5.

Sowing

Once soil temperatures reach 7°C (45°F) leek seeds can be direct sown 15mm (½in) deep, in rows

The planting holes for young leeks are filled with water, not soil

Drain pipes being used to blanch leeks

Blanched leek

Stopping a leek from bolting by removing the flower bud

30cm (12in) apart, thinned out at the 2 to 3 leaf stage to 7 to 15cm (3 to 6in) according to the size of leek required. Leeks are also raised in a seed bed or a greenhouse and transplanted.

Spacing

For maximum yield of normal sized leeks, allow 15cm (6in) between the plants and 30cm(1ft) between the rows, this allows just about enough room to earth up for blanching. If a raised bed is used, together with pipes for blanching, maximum yield can be obtained by planting 22cm (9in) in a square pattern. The size of transplant affects the final size of the leek, large transplants produce large leeks, small transplants produce small leeks. Putting two or three leek plants per station instead of one will produce small thin leeks without much loss of yield.

Transplanting

A hole is made at each station with a dibber (or a rake upside-down) to a depth of 15cm (6in).

A young leek plant is placed in each hole with half of its leaf below ground. The hole is then filled with water. Unlike other transplants the **hole is not filled with soil**. In some areas of the country half the length of both the leaves and roots of leek transplants are cut off before planting. There is no evidence that this practice is helpful. However if the roots are so long that they reduce the planting depth

they can be trimmed back without causing any harm.

Fertilising

Four weeks after planting 10% nitrogen fertiliser is applied at the rate of 150g per sq m (4oz per sq yd). This can either be spread in dry form on the surface or watered on with a rose can.

Watering.

In dry weather transplanted leeks will require watering each week until they are established. A small amount (½ litre[1 pt] per 5 plants) applied at the base of the plant is sufficient. Further watering is not normally required.

Blanching

The aim of the grower is to produce a long, white shank (stem). This is achieved by excluding the light. The traditional method of blanching was to sow seeds in the bottom of a 'V' shaped drill which was gradually filled in as the plants grew. Later, soil is drawn in in between the rows until they are growing in an inverted 'V' shaped ridge. This method is effective but great care is needed to prevent soil from dropping inside the leaves. An easier method is to grow on the flat and blanch by sliding a short length of scrap plastic piping over each plant.

Bolting

Leeks will sometimes run to seed,

especially if the young plants were subject to a long period of cold weather. When this happens the emerging flowers are cut off and the leek is left to grow.

Harvesting

Leeks are harvested as required throughout autumn and winter, any which have begun to bolt are taken first. A garden fork is used to lever the plant with one hand whilst the other hand holds the leek by the shank and pulls it up. Roots are trimmed off with a knife and the shank is cleaned by removing the outside leaf.

Succession

In order to harvest leeks from September until April, three different varieties are sown.

Star Varieties
(in order of maturity)

King Richard
The 30cm (12in) shank gives a high yield.
Albinstar
A long shank with slight bulbing.
Wintra
Short shank with little bulbing
Matures January to March.

Cooking

Cut into rings 2cm (1in) thick and steam until tender. Baby leeks (ie the small leeks produced by planting three or more leek plants per station) are best cooked whole and served with a sauce.

Grower's Timetable – LEEK	
Autumn	Dig and manure the soil.
March	Sow seeds of an early variety thinly in trays in a cold frame or cold greenhouse.
April	When the soil has warmed sow seeds of two later varieties thinly along drills 30 cm (12in) apart at a depth of 1.5cm (in).
May	Thin seedlings to 15cm (6in) apart.
	Transplant early variety 15cm (6in) apart, along rows 30cm (12in) apart.
June	Top dress with 10% nitrogen at the rate of 150g per sq m (4oz per sq yd).
	Blanch by earthing up or covering individual plants with short lengths of pipe.
	Control weeds.
July/	
September	Remove the flower buds from any which bolt. Control weeds.
September/	
March	Harvest as required.

LETTUCE
Lactuca sativa

Bred from a wild form, which grows in the areas around Iran, the lettuce has been cultivated for over 6,000 years. The original forms were all loose leaf types, as hearted lettuce did not appear until the sixteenth century. Lettuce is now grown throughout the world, although some areas are restricted to leaf lettuce, as hearts do not form when the mean temperature is over 21°C (70°F). In the UK, by a combination of different varieties and sowing dates, it is possible to have garden lettuce available for a large part of the year. For details of this – see varieties on page 96.

Types of Lettuce
1. Butterhead. A heart forming type with soft, delicate leaves. Seeds of butterhead lettuce will not germinate at temperatures in excess of 24°C (78°F).

2. Crisphead. The leaves of crispheads are succulent, crisp and wrinkled. The hearts are usually larger than those of butterheads.

3. Cos. A cos lettuce forms an upright elongated heart. The leaves are long, crisp and sweet. Some varieties of cos need tying with string around the top to encourage heart formation. Cos lettuces are slower to mature than the other types.

4. Loose leaf. These types do not form hearts and individual leaves can be picked as required.

Most loose leaf varieties have soft, curled leaves but varieties are now available with crisp leaves.

Cos varieties of lettuce can also be grown as loose-leaf types. Heart formation is prevented by very close planting.

Some varieties of lettuce have been bred for winter greenhouse production. If these are sown in summer they will bolt without hearting.

Soil
Any free draining, moisture retentive soil will support a crop of lettuce. The ideal pH is 6.5 to 7.5.

Methods of Growing
There are three common methods of growing outdoor hearted lettuce.

1. Sow in pots in a cold frame (or cold greenhouse) in February. Transplant under cloches or fleece during April. The first heads should be ready by the end of May.

2. Sow in drills in the open ground at three week intervals from April to July. Thin out (and hand weed) to 30cm (12in).

3. Sow the variety Valdor under cloches or frames in October; the young plants will survive the winter and produce hearts in early May.

In very mild districts the variety Winter Density, sown in September, will survive the winter without protection.

Sowing
The earliest lettuces are grown from plants which are raised indoors. During summer, lettuces do not transplant well and are most easily grown by sowing seeds in rows and thinning out. The soil is raked to a fine tilth and drills are drawn 1cm (in) deep. The bottoms of the drills are watered and seeds are sprinkled very thinly along the length of each drill. The drills are then back filled and gently firmed with the head of a rake. High soil temperatures in summer may prevent butterhead varieties from germinating, the temperature can be kept down with cold water and shade until the seeds have germinated.

Spacing
Planting distances vary with the variety, small types like Tom Thumb obviously require less space than large types like Webbs Wonderful. Most hearting and loose leaf types are planted 30cm (12in) apart along rows that are also 30cm (12in) apart. For leaf production from cos varieties the rows are 13cm (5in) apart and the lettuces are thinned to only 2cm (1in) apart.

Fertilising
Before planting or sowing, rake 10% nitrogen fertiliser into the soil at the rate of 100g per sq m (3oz per sq yd).

Watering
Watering improves both the size and quality of lettuce. During periods of low rainfall, water twice each week giving 11 litres per sq m (2gal per sq yd) each time. If water is in short supply, give a single watering of 22 litres per sq m (4gal per sq yd) 10 days before harvest.

Sparrows
Early in the season sparrows find young lettuce plants irresistible and make short work of both seedlings and transplants. Fleece, chicken wire or some other form of protection is essential. This protection is not needed later in the season.

Harvest
Lettuces are ready for harvesting as soon as the hearts are firm, test by applying gentle pressure to the top with the finger tips. To harvest simply cut the lettuce off at soil level with a sharp knife.

Lettuce ready for harvest

Young lettuce being protected from slugs by the means of a beer trap

Storing

After harvesting place the lettuce in an open plastic bag and store in a refrigerator until required. This method keeps the lettuce crisp and fresh for well over a week. Only wash the amount of lettuce required for immediate use; as washed lettuce soon discolours and becomes unpalatable.

Star Varieties

Butterheads:

Avondefiance
Crops from June to August, withstands dry periods. Resistant to root aphid.

Reskia
Crops from June to October, fairly

resistant to downy mildew.

Crispheads:

Lakeland
Good for cropping in frames as well as outside, resistant to root aphid and mildew.

Saladin
Crops from July to September, large heads, slow to bolt.

Cos:

Little Gem
Small hearts of excellent flavour. Space 15cm (6in) apart along the row.

Looseleaf:

Lollo Rossa
Crinkled red tinged leaf, very at-

tractive with a mild flavour.

Lollo Bionda
Similar to Rossa but with pale green leaves.

Salad Bowl
Stands for several weeks, two sowings will give continuity for most of the summer.

Others:

Valdor
For autumn sowing (will fail if sown at other times)

Kellys
Crisp hearts, sow November to January in a cold greenhouse or polytunnel, inside cropping.

Grower's Timetable – LETTUCE	
Hearted lettuces do not stand; only sow a small area at a time.	
February	Sow butterhead variety in pots in a cold frame or cold greenhouse.
April	Transplant from cold frame to open ground, 30 x 30cm (12 x 12in). Protect from sparrows.
	Sow butterhead and loose leaf varieties in open ground.
May	Sow crisphead variety.
May - July	Control weeds.
	Water regularly in dry weather.
	Thin out to 30cm (12in apart) for large types and 15cm (6in) for small types.
	Sow butterhead and crisphead varieties when previous sowings are almost ready for thinning.
	Make a second sowing of a looseleaf variety.
October	Sow the variety Valdor under cloches or in a cold frame.

MARROWS
see Courgette

MANGETOUT
see Peas

MINT
Mentha spicata
This herb is included here as no vegetable garden should be without a supply of mint. Mint was brought to this country by the Romans and soon became one of the most popular herbs. A perennial

This mint is contained in a wooden box to stop it from spreading

plant which is grown for its aromatic leaves; it spreads rapidly by means of rhizomes (underground stems) and can become very invasive. Mint flowers are attractive to bees.

Soil

Unlike most herbs mint will grow in partial shade. It tolerates a wide range of soils and can be grown in almost any type of garden soil, providing that it does not become waterlogged. Once established mint quickly spreads and soon becomes a nuisance, the best way to prevent this is to surround the plants with

a ring of plastic pressed 15cm (6in) into the soil and protruding 5cm (2in) above. A ring cut from an old oil drum or similar is ideal.

Sowing and planting

Mint is easily grown from seeds. These are sown in situ 1cm (½in) deep into a fine tilth. The young shoots should not be harvested during the first year while the plants are becoming established.

If grown inside a ring of plastic, the centre of the plant tends to die out during the second year with all the growth around the edges. This is overcome by digging up the plant, saving a few lengths of its rhizomes and replanting these in the centre of the ring. The remainder of the plant is discarded. Replanting during March or April every second year produces a permanent supply of mint from a fully controlled plant.

Fertilising

If fresh soil is introduced each time mint is replanted there is no need to fertilise.

Watering

Watering is only necessary in drought conditions; sufficient water should then be given to wet the soil to a depth of 30cm (12in) this is repeated at 2 or 3 week intervals.

Winter Supply.

A supply of fresh mint is easily

obtained in winter. A 18cm (7in) plant pot (or other container) is filled with compost to within 5cm (2in) of the top. Half a dozen pieces, each 10cm (4in) long, of **freshly dug** rhizome are laid on the compost. The pot is then filled with compost and watered. In a warm greenhouse or kitchen, shoots will be ready for use within three or four weeks.

Harvest

Young shoots or leaves are picked as required.

Above left: Mint rhizomes before covering with compost. If this is done in October a winter crop is assured

Above right: Mint left to flower attracts a lot of pollinating insects into the garden

ONIONS

Allium cepa

The onion is a biennial that stores food in a fleshy bulb during its first growing season and flowers during its second growing season. The onion is harvested half way through its life cycle for its edible fleshy bulb. People have grown onions for over 5,000 years and they are the second most important culinary vegetable. Leaves are also edible and are used in salads as 'spring onions', the leaves which sprout from stored onions in early spring are also eaten in this way.

The onion plant is fairly frost hardy but several days of low temperatures will cause it to bolt. The development of an onion is dependant upon day length, during short days leaves are produced, but once the days are 16 hours long a bulb begins to develop. When bulbing starts, a plant with a large amount of leaf will produce a large bulb but a plant with a small amount of leaf can only produce a small bulb. This knowledge is used by some growers to produce very large bulbs and by other growers

to produce very small ones – onion sets.

Onion Sets

Onion seeds sown during the second half of May produce a crop of very small onions. An onion that is less than 15mm in diameter is sexually immature and if planted will grow into a larger onion. These small onions are called 'sets'. It is possible to have sets with a diameter larger than 15mm (½in) but they have to be stored throughout the winter at temperatures of over 25°C (77°F). Buying and planting onion sets is by far the easiest way of growing a crop of onions. When buying onion sets from garden centres, choose small ones as they are less likely to blot than larger ones.

Onion Pips

Onions can also be grown from 'pips'. These are produced by planting an onion in spring and leaving it to flower. The flower buds are shaved off just before the flowers open. A number of small bulblets grow where the flowers would have been. When the

bulblets ripen they are stored and grown the following season in the same way as onion sets.

Soil

Onions are subject to a number of soil borne pests and diseases and they should be grown in the same area only one year in three. The leaves are easily damaged by wind and on windy sites they will benefit from some protection.

Good, fertile, well-drained soil with a pH of 6.5 or more is ideal. In practice the pH of the soil should be checked a year earlier and lime added if necessary. The soil should be high in organic matter. This is achieved by digging in well rotted manure or compost. The onion bed is best prepared in autumn and left open to winter frosts. In spring a tilth is produced by raking, light soils should be firmed by treading just once before the final raking.

Spacing

Spacing has a considerable effect on the total yield and the size of onions. Wide spacing produces large onions and a small yield

Onion sets being grown from seed

Onions grown close together produce a heavy yield of small bulbs

Onions tied by their tops to a rope will remain in good condition throughout the winter

whilst closer spacing produces medium sized onions and a large yield (there are so many more onions). For maximum yield of medium sized bulbs the plants are spaced 5cm (2in) apart along rows 25cm (10in) apart.

Bulbs required for pickling are grown from seed and thinned to 1 cm (½ in) apart with 30cm (1ft) between the rows.

Fertilising

A well prepared onion bed will contain all the necessary plant foods for a good yield. Yields will however be increased by encouraging extra leaf growth before the plants begin to bulb in late May by applying extra nitrogen. A top dressing of 100g of 10% nitrogen fertiliser for each square metre of bed (3oz per sq yd) is the maximum and should not be exceeded. On onion beds which were not well

prepared the top dresssing of nitrogen is replaced with a foliar feed of either Phostrogen or Miraclegro. In order that the correct amount is given, the foliar feed is mixed in a watering can and applied according to manufacturer's instructions – automatic feeders on the ends of hosepipes do not give enough control and excess nitrogen is harmful.

Watering

Onions are deep rooted and require little watering. If the weather is dry during spring and early summer a limited amount of water is given to establish the plants. Onions should not be watered after the mid July as ripening will be delayed and the bulbs will not store well.

Weeds

Onion leaves are thin and give little shade to smother weeds. Weed control is therefore very important – especially during the early stages of growth. Growing onions from plants or sets, instead of direct sowing, considerably reduces the amount of weeding.

Harvesting

Onions harvested before the end of August keep better than those harvested later in the season. In mid August the tops bend over naturally, this stops growth and exposes the bulbs to more sunlight. To speed this process a fork is pushed into the ground a few centimetres away from the bulbs which are gently eased upwards to damage the roots.

Two weeks later lift the bulbs and lay them on the soil to ripen, in wet weather they will ripen more quickly if raised above the soil on an inverted tray or a horizontal net. When the leaves are brown the onions can be transferred to a permanent store.

Storing

An onion is a natural storage organ that keeps well throughout the

winter. When the dormant period ends in spring, the bulb grows leaves and becomes unsuitable for the kitchen. Dormancy is broken by warmth and damp, the aim therefore is to keep the bulbs dry and cold. This is best done by tying the bulbs in ropes or reeves and hanging them in a cold airy shed. On no account should onions be put into plastic bags as the resulting dampness will cause the roots to grow.

Frost does no damage until the temperature falls below -3°C (27°F), in most areas very little frost protection is needed.

Only store perfect onions as damaged and thick-necked bulbs do not store well.

Autumn Sown Onions

In May and June stored onions have finished and the new season's crop is not ready. This gap in the supply is filled by growing Japanese onions which over-winter as small plants and mature in early summer. It is important to sow these onions at the correct time as if sown too early they run to seed and if sown too late they are not large enough to stand through the winter. The ideal sowing date varies from the first week of August in the north of Britain to the end of August in the south. Onions do not germinate well above 21°C (70°F) if soil temperatures are higher water the drill with cold water and cover with a reflective material like white plastic or cooking foil. Japanese onions are less likely to bolt if given a light dressing of nitrogen fertiliser each month throughout the winter.

Japanese onions do not store well and are used within 2 months of harvest.

Japanese onion sets are also available and these are planted 3 weeks later than the sowing time for seeds. Both seeds and sets are likely to fail on very heavy soil and poorly drained soil.

Note shallots keep for longer periods than onions and these can be used to bridge the gap from June to July when home grown onions are not available.

Star varieties

Spring sown:
Hygro
Brown, vigorous grower, globe shaped.
Southport red globe
Purple/red, globe shaped.

Autumn sown:
Buffalo:
High yield, globe shaped bulbs.
Senshyu Semi-Globe Yellow:
High yield, globe shaped, three weeks later than Buffalo.

Cooking
To serve with grills:
Peel off the layers of dead skin, slice across into rings 1cm (½in) thick, chop the rings into chunks, microwave on high until tender. Fry in a little oil.
To serve as a vegetable: Peel medium sized onions, cook in boiling salted water for half an hour. Drain and place in a casserole dish. Add bouquet garni and half cover with stock. Braise with the lid on until tender. Reg5 290°C 375°F

Growing Very Large Onions
There is considerable interest in the growing of very large onions.

This is sometimes competitive with prize money, but more often it is just for fun. The added bonus is that the large onions are delicious to eat raw or they can be used to replace normal onions in cooking. A part used onion keeps perfectly well in a fridge with a little clingfilm over the cut section.

Some well-known growers use the same onion bed year after year with success, sooner or later however they will fail for the reasons given on page 15.

Only certain varieties will achieve weights of over 5lb (the world record is over 11lbs!). Most seed companies offer a suitable variety, Kelsae and Mammoth are probably the best known of these. Kings have a superb variety called 'Monkston' which is giving excellent results.

How To Grow A Large Onion.
• Purchase seeds of a suitable variety.
• Select an open sunny airy and well drained site
• In autumn dig in lots of well rotted manure or other suitable organic matter, making sure that it is well mixed with the soil.
• Check the pH, it needs to be 6.75 – 7.25 and add lime if necessary.
• If site and soil are unsuitable use a top quality grobag and grow only

two onions per bag.
• During the second half of December sow seeds individually in 7.5cm (3in) pots. Use a top quality compost either multipurpose or freshly made John Innes No.1.
• Germinate in a propagator set at 20°C (68°F).
• When at the crook stage (ie the seedling looks like a hairpin) transfer from the propagator to a greenhouse shelf where the light is good. Grow on at 16°C as far as possible but do not let the temperature fall below 10°C.
• Keep moist but do not over-water. Ventilate as often as possible

Large onions need to be widely spaced in order to reach maximum weight. The size is compared with a 50 pence piece

Grower's Timetable – ONIONS	
Autumn	Prepare onion bed by digging in manure or compost. Leave surface rough and lumpy.
March	(or early April) Rake the soil to a medium tilth.
March	(or early April) Plant onion *sets firmly just under the soil surface with the tips just visible. Space the sets 5cm (2in) apart along the row and 25cm (10in) between the rows. In some gardens, sets are pulled up by sparrows, this problem is easily overcome by covering the bed with fleece or by burying the sets completely.
May	Top dress with a high nitrogen fertiliser – Chempak Number 2 or similar.
May/July	Keep free from weeds by regular use of the dutch hoe (care! onions produce fine feeding roots near to the surface) Remove the flower bud from any which begin to bolt.
May/June	In very dry weather water every 2 weeks, do not water after mid July.
June	Give a liquid feed of Phostrogen or Miraclegro. Wet the leaves as well as the soil.
August	Ease plants up with a fork and harvest two weeks later.
September	Tie into ropes and hang in a dry, airy building.

*Note: Onions can also be grown from seeds or plants. Sow seeds thinly along the row and thin out to the recommended spacings as soon as the seedlings are large enough to handle (or leave a little longer and use the thinnings as salad onions).

and give additional light (a fluorescent tube is ideal). **Do not give light for too long as the plants must have at least 9 hours' darkness every night.**
• When the roots reach the edge of the pot, pot on into 12.5cm (5in) pots using freshly made John Innes No. 3 or a top quality potting compost.
• In early April harden off with care. (see glossary).
• In mid April rake into the onion bed a general purpose fertiliser

(10:10:10) at the rate of 120g per sq m (3 oz per sq yd). The bed should be firm with a fine tilth on top.
• At the end of April, water the plants with Miraclegro or Phostrogen and then plant out allowing 37cm (15in) between plants. Take extreme care not to disturb the roots. Make sure that the hole is large enough, the aim is to cover the white part with 1cm (½in) of soil.
• Protect from the wind with a fleece surround.

• Three weeks after planting out give a light dressing (25g per sq m) 3/4g per sq yd of nitrate of soda and repeat each fortnight during June and July, regular foliar feeding with Phostrogen or Miraclegro during alternate weeks.
• In mid-August and again in early September give light dressings (25g per sq m) ¾g per sq yd of sulphate of potash.
• Harvest in mid-September.

ONIONS, SALAD
Allium cepa
Salad onions take longer to come to maturity than most other salads, but they produce their crop over a longer period. It is possible to have salad onions ready with the first crop of lettuce by sowing a winter hardy crop.

Sowing
Seeds are sown in a firm seed bed with a fine tilth 12mm (½in) deep. Seeds are sown in bands rather than drills, a sowing rate of 40 seeds per 30cm length of a band 8 cm wide (40 seeds per foot length of a band 3 in wide) will give maximum yield. The seeds are distributed evenly in the bottom of the band.

Spacing
Salad onions are grown from seeds, sown directly into the soil. For maximum yields seeds are sown in bands 8cm (3in) wide with

22cm (9in) between the rows. Sowing in a wide band instead of a single row reduces inter crop competition, giving more and larger sized plants – it also increases the amount of hand weeding! However as only small areas are sown at any one time the task is not arduous.

Watering
When sowing in dry weather, the open drill (or band) should be well watered before the seeds are sown. If dry weather persists, apply sufficient water each week to thoroughly wet the soil. A rose can is best for this purpose.

Harvesting
Individual onions are selectively harvested, the largest plants are taken leaving the others to grow. A single sowing will provide onions over a 4 week period before bulbing starts. Any unharvested

plants can be left to form bulbs and used for culinary purposes.

Succession
It is possible to have salad onions available from April until October. A winter hardy variety is sown during the latter half of August or early in September. Half of this sowing is advanced by applying cloches from February. Three sowings one in March, one in April and the last at the end of May will supply fresh salad onions throughout the summer until October.

Star Varieties
Winter Hardy White Lisbon
For sowing in the autumn.

White Lisbon
Develops bulbs more slowly than the winter hardy type.

Caution: White Lisbon is not sufficiently hardy to stand the winter.

PARSLEY
Petroselinum crispum
A biennial herb which is a native of southern Europe. It is tolerant of a wide range of environmental conditions and is grown almost worldwide. The leaves and stems are used for flavouring and its leaves are used to garnish. Parsley has a large tap-root and one form, Hamburg Parsley, is grown for its root that is used in winter in a similar

way to parsnips. Parsley is best grown as an annual; there is only a small crop in the second year before the plants begin to flower.

Soil
Unlike most herbs parsley requires a deep, rich moisture retentive soil and performs very badly on light, acid soils. A pH between 5.5 and 7.0 is necessary. Parsley grows well in full sun but will also toler-

ate a little shade. In common with other herbs parsley is best situated as near to the kitchen door as possible. A fine tilth is required for outside sowing.

Sowing and planting
Parsley has an undeserved reputation as a difficult plant to germinate. For successful germination a little light is needed, it is far better to raise the plants indoors and

transplant, than to sow outdoors. A tray, preferably a divided one, is filled with multi-purpose compost and well watered. One parsley seed is placed in the middle of each section and pressed into the surface with the point of a pencil to a depth of 2mm (1/16in). The tray is then placed inside a plastic bag and kept on a warm window cill. When seedlings are in second leaf, they can be hardened off by putting outside in the day time and inside at night for a few days. After this time they are planted up in the garden.

Sowings can also be made directly into the soil at a depth of 1cm (1/2in). As parsley germinates more slowly than most weeds it is important that weed seedlings are weeded out regularly.

Spacing

Parsley may be grown in rows but is most usually planted in a square bed alongside the path for convenient access. A good crop is obtained by spacing plants 10cm (4in) apart in both directions. Hamburg parsley requires double this spacing to allow for root development.

Fertilising

As with most leaf crops, a top dressing of nitrogen fertiliser is beneficial. Apply 70g per sq m (2oz per sq yd) of 10% nitrogen soon after the plants have become established.

Watering

It is very important to keep a parsley seed bed moist until the seeds germinate. Parsley has a deep taproot and will only require additional water in very dry conditions. Apply 15l litres per sq m (3gal per sq yd) every 2 or 3 weeks.

Carrot Root Fly

Carrot root fly larvae will attack parsley, when this pest is present the leaves begin to turn a reddish pink. For control measures turn to page 49.

Harvest

Harvest can begin when a plant has seven or eight leaves and continue at intervals throughout the summer. The leaves are picked complete with the stalk, no more than half the leaves should be taken from any plant at any one time. A mid-summer sowing can be covered with cloches in the autumn to extend harvest up until the end of the year.

Star Varieties

Moss curled
The best variety for garnish.

Plain-leaved
Flat leaves, not very attractive for garnish but a strong flavour.

Hamburg
Leaves may be used but grown mainly for its parsnip like roots.

Freezing
Parsley freezes exceptionally well and, when thawed out, is indistinguishable from fresh. Wash the leaves and chop them to the required size. Spread on a tray and freeze. Once frozen transfer the parsley to a box and store in the freezer.

Parsley variety Moss Curled

Parsley and Hamburg parsley compared

Grower's Timetable – PARSLEY	
March	Fill a divided tray with compost and sow one seed in each section, press it just under the surface with a pencil. Germinate in a propagator or window cill.
May	Harden off and plant outside in a block with 10cm (4in) between the plants.
June	Keep weed free. Water if necessary. Harvest regularly as soon as plants have eight leaves.
July	Make a second sowing in the same way as the first, or insitu in the soil.
July -	Continue weed control.
October	Harvest as required and freeze any surplus.
October	Cover the second sowing with cloches to provide fresh parsley up until Christmas.

PARSNIP
Pastinaca sativa

The parsnip is a hardy biennial which is grown as an annual for its edible root. It is a native of this country and has been cultivated since Roman times.

Soil
A deep well-cultivated soil with no stones is ideal. Well-rotted manure or compost thoroughly mixed into the soil will improve yield and will not cause roots to fork. Parsnips tolerate any pH between 5.5 and 7.

A satisfactory crop can be obtained on some unsuitable soils by making a wide tapering slit with a spade, filling it with compost or fine soil and sowing on the top. If this method is used care should be taken not to compact the surrounding soil. Growers of exhibition parsnips use a similar method that involves making deep holes with a crowbar. Heavy soils which are likely to become waterlogged need to be organised into raised beds with the addition of sand and/or peat.

Sowing

Very early sowings are often recommended for this crop, however little is to be gained by putting seeds into cold soil and early sowings often produce erratic results. In addition some parsnip seeds are undeveloped and this delays their germination. If soil temperatures are below 7°C (45°F) germination is extremely slow. Warming the soil with a sheet of clear plastic for a week or so before sowing increases the chance of success. The plastic sheet is left in position until the seedlings have two true leaves. To avoid water stress the sheet is removed during damp rather than sunny weather. It follows that the temperature of the soil, rather than the date should govern the time of sowing parsnips. Seeds are sown thinly along each row 1cm (½in) deep.

Spacing

For maximum yield the spacing of parsnips varies according to variety. Large rooted varieties like Offenham require twice the space of small rooted varieties like Avonresister. For large varieties 30cm (1ft) between the rows with 15cm (6in) between the plants is ideal. For small varieties 2cm (8in) between the rows with 8cm (3in) between the plants will give maximum yield. The spacing between plants is obtained by thinning as soon as the seedlings are large enough to handle.

Fertilising

Apply 70g per sq m (2oz per sq yd) of 10% nitrogen fertiliser as a top dressing when the plants have two true leaves.

Watering

Too much water produces leaf growth at the expense of root growth. In dry weather, water is given once every two weeks at the rate of 5 litres per sq m (1gal per sq yd) at the early stages of growth and 16 litres per sq m (3gal per sq yd) to the more mature crop. The soil is not allowed to dry out, as rain after a long, dry spell will cause the roots to split.

Harvest

Parsnips are dug up with a garden fork. The fork is inserted several centimetres away from the root and pushed vertically downwards as far as it will go. One hand grasps the base of the leaves and pulls gently, whilst the other hand uses the fork as a lever. If the fork is not pushed in to the soil far enough the root will be damaged. Roots are lifted throughout the winter as and when required.

Storing

Parsnips are very hardy and are best stored in the ground where they have grown. In cold districts a covering of soil over the crowns to a depth of 8cm (3in) should give adequate protection. Cold weather makes parsnips taste better as some of the starch they contain is converted into sugar.

Star Varieties

Avonresister
Small, sweet bulbous roots with a good resistance to canker.

Harvesting parsnips

Grower's Timetable – PARSNIP	
Autumn	Deeply work the soil and mix in well rotted manure or compost.
End March/Early April	Sow seeds 1cm (½in) deep in rows 30cm (1ft) apart for large varieties and 20cm (8in) apart for small varieties.
May	Thin large varieties to 15cm (6in) and small varieties to 8cm (3in) apart along the row.
	Dutch hoe to control weeds where necessary.
All summer	In dry weather do not allow soil to dry out.
	Water every two weeks.
December	In cold districts cover with 8cm (3in) of soil.
Winter	Harvest as required.

White Gem
Large wedge shaped roots with a good resistance to canker.

Cooking
The roots are trimmed and scrubbed clean. They are cut lengthways into quarters and if the centre core is tough it is removed with the point of a sharp knife. Cut into pieces and boil with the lid on until tender. Drain and serve with butter or in a sauce.

Parsnip quarters may be roasted in an oven in a little fat or with a joint. They are also very useful in casseroles.

Peas are best grown in triple rows. The seeds here will be covered with a light raking

PEAS
Pisum sativum
Peas are annuals which are grown for their edible seeds and the pods of certain varieties. The species originated in Central Asia but it has disappeared from the wild. Ripe pea seeds have been eaten for centuries but the eating of fresh peas did not become common in this country until after the fifteenth century. Pea flowers readily self-pollinate and insects are not necessary for pod formation.

Mangetout and Sugar Snaps
Mangetout and sugar snaps are grown in exactly the same way as peas. They are both harvested just before the pods begin to swell, the pods are then eaten whole. Mangetout have succulent flat pods whilst sugar snaps have thick fleshy pods. If picked regularly mangetout produce very large crops, but if they are left to develop, the resulting peas are not very palatable. If sugar snaps are left to develop the pods become inedible but the peas can be shelled out and used.

The Site
An open site with plenty of sunshine and little wind is the ideal. The same site should not be used more than one year in three as a precaution against soil borne pests and diseases.

Soil Conditions
Peas require a moisture retentive soil with a pH of between 6.0 and 7.5. As the seeds are large, raking to a very fine tilth is unnecessary and should be avoided. A mulch applied when the plants are small is beneficial.

Fertilising
Peas growing in well managed soil do not require any additional nitrogen. Bacteria in the root nodules convert atmospheric nitrogen into a form which is available to the plant.

Sowing
Although the pea plant is fairly hardy the seed does not germinate readily below temperatures of 10°C (50°F). Peas sown in cold soil often fail because of soil borne disease or mice. Early crops are obtained by germinating seeds in a greenhouse in a length of rain gutter filled with compost. The gutter of young plants is placed in a shallow trench and the gutter is then slid away.

As soon as soil temperatures rise peas are sown in a trench 3.5cm (1in) deep and covered with soil.

Spacing
Spacing depends upon whether the pods are going to be picked a number of times over a period or just once at a single picking. Where a single destructive picking is intended, a short variety is sown spacing the seeds about 5cm (2in) apart in a flat bottomed trench 15cm (6in) wide. A 30cm (2ft) path either side is left for access. Short varieties grown for a single picking are not staked.

If the crop is to be harvested over two or three weeks, a taller variety like Cavalier is sown. Peas are sown in bands of three rows 11cm (4 in) apart with individual seeds placed 11cm apart along the row. This spacing gives the maximum yield.

Where peas are grown in raised beds the rows should run across the width of the bed and not along the length. This gives better use of space and makes picking easier.

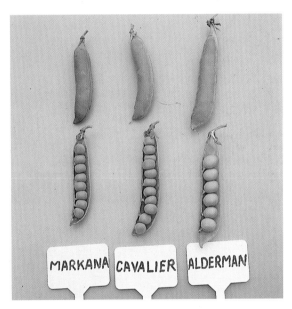

Markham, Cavalier and Alderman peas compared

Watering
Watering young pea plants will increase the growth stems and leaves but will not increase the number or size of pods. Watering at flowering time however will increase the yield considerably. Water should be **applied to the soil** along the

Hurst Greenshaft – an excellent variety for main crop production

Peas on a net

Taller varieties should be staked with twiggy sticks or a net, supported by strings along both sides of the row.

Harvest

When peas are fully grown they begin to ripen, this process reduces the amount of water in the peas and they become hard. Peas do not keep in prime condition on the plant for more than a few days. Full pods are picked and the flatter ones left on the plant to fill. Picking is best carried out with the minimum of disturbance to the plant, this involves using two hands, one to support the stem and the other to remove the pod. Pulling up the plants during the final picking ensures that no pods are left behind.

If dry peas are required the pods are left on the plant until they turn brown and the seeds become hard. These are then gathered at a single picking.

Succession

It is very difficult to obtain a succession of peas as the time taken to reach maturity is weather dependent. Three rows of the same variety, sown at fortnightly intervals are likely to crop all at once. A single sowing on one day of three varieties with different maturity times is a more reliable method of obtaining succession. The sowing

of three varieties at the beginning of May, the end of May and mid June gives the best chance of fresh peas throughout the summer. Sowing an early variety at the end of June may give a later crop depending upon the amount of autumn sunshine.

A crop as early as May can be obtained by sowing smooth seeded varieties in October or November and over-wintering under cloches. This is only possible on light well drained soils.

Star Varieties

Mangetout:
Carouby de Maussanne
Purple flowers, excellent texture, heavy cropper. Height 1.7m (5ft).

Sugar Snaps:
Sugar Snap
Good flavour, heavy cropper. Height 2m (6ft).

Smooth seeded:
Feltham First
Good crop of large peas, flavour not as good as wrinkle seeded varieties. Height 45cm (18in).

Early:
Beagle
Very reliable Height 45cm (18in).

Maincrop:

rows at the rate of 8l per sq m (1gal per sq yd) twice a week throughout the flowering and pod swelling period.

Support

Varieties up to 60cm (2ft) are not usually staked as they support each other with their tendrils.

Grower's Timetable – PEAS	
March/April	As soon as the soil is warm rake to a medium tilth.
	Rake out a flat bottomed trench 3.5cm (1in) deep and 23cm (9in) wide.
	Sprinkle seeds of an early variety in the trench with about 4cm (2in) between them.
	Gently press the seeds into the soil with the sole of one foot, or the head of a rake.
	Back fill the trench by carefully raking soil over the seeds.
	Cover with fleece to protect from birds.
May	Sow a main crop variety. Sow three rows with just 11cm (4in) between them, place the seeds 11cm (4in) apart along the rows.
	Arrange a support along the triple row, to the height stated on the seed packet. This support can be dead twigs, strings stretched between stakes or a large mesh plastic net - either side of the row.
June	When the peas begin to flower give the soil a good soaking. Repeat twice each week during dry weather.
	Towards the end of the month make a second sowing of an early variety.
July/August	Harvest the pods as soon as they are full. As soon as harvest is complete, pull up and compost the plants.

Hurst Greenshaft
Large well-filled pods, excellent flavour.

Cavalier
Produces pods over a long period. Height 75cm (2ft 6in).

Cooking

Put a little sugar and a sprig of mint into a pan of water and bring to the boil. Drop in freshly podded peas and simmer until tender.

Prepare Mangetout and sugar snaps by removing the stalk* and rubbing off the remains of the flower, wash and cook in boiling water until tender.

*Remove only the smallest amount of pod with the stalk, if too much pod is taken the pea will open during cooking. Mangetout is an ideal vegetable to add to a stir-fry.

Freezing

If only young peas are frozen the 'garden pea' flavour is retained.

Blanch for 30 seconds by dropping into boiling water. Drain and transfer to cold water. Drain and remove any surplus water with kitchen towel. Spread on metal trays and freeze. When the peas are frozen store them in a plastic container.

Mangetout and sugar snaps are frozen in the same way except that the blanching time is increased to one minute.

Mangetout showing development from flower to seed. The pencil indicates the best stage to harvest

POTATO

Solanum tuberosum

Potatoes have been cultivated in South America for over 2,000 years, they were first brought to Europe in 1587. Potatoes became the staple crop in Ireland and much of Northern Europe and an epidemic of potato blight during 1845 and 1846 caused widespread famine in Ireland. Potato plants are half hardy and are destroyed at temperatures below -1°C (30°F).

'New' Potatoes or 'Early' Potatoes.

Home grown early potatoes are far superior to purchased ones and fresh dug new potatoes are such a culinary delight that this crop should feature in every vegetable garden. The early harvest allows time for a salad or transplanted brassica crop to be taken from the same area. New potatoes are grown from varieties that produce tubers within 12 weeks of planting. The new tubers are lifted before they mature, at this stage the skins are thin and easily scraped off. New potatoes must be eaten as soon as possible after lifting, otherwise they dehydrate, their sugars convert to starch and the superb flavour is lost.

Maincrop Potatoes

Main crop potatoes are grown from higher yielding varieties that take longer to mature. They are harvested after the tops die down and the skins on the tubers have toughened. When properly harvested and stored, maincrop potatoes will keep in good condition until May.

Farm grown maincrop potatoes are usually cheap and this crop is seldom worth growing by most amateurs. Maincrop potatoes can be useful to clean a very weedy area or to rest an area from brassicas where crop rotation has failed. Gardeners with wet clay

Early potatoes chitting in the light

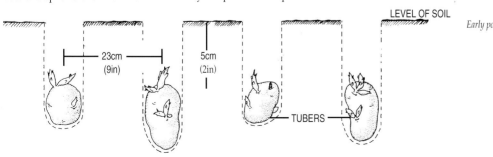

LEVEL OF SOIL

23cm (9in)

5cm (2in)

TUBERS

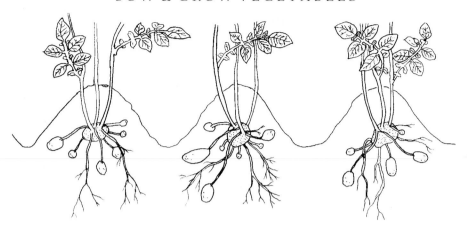

soils are warned that maincrop potatoes are very subject to slug damage.

Soil

In order to keep potato scab to a minimum, potatoes are the last crop in the rotation when pH is at its lowest point. The soil is deeply dug and well manured. As a fine tilth is not required raking is kept to the minimum.

Fertilising

Potatoes require high levels of potash. After planting rake in a compound fertiliser like Chempak No 4 (15:15:30) at a rate of 100g per sq m (3oz sq yd) for earlies and 160g per sq metre (5oz per sq yd) for the maincrop.

Potatoes need to be grown on ridges otherwise the tubers emerge and turn green

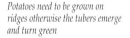

Care of Tubers

Potatoes are grown from tubers known as 'seed' potatoes. In the UK most tubers contain virus diseases that are transmitted by aphids. For this reason 'seed' potatoes can only be grown in the parts of the country that are relatively aphid free. Gardeners are strongly advised to buy new 'seed' potatoes each year, or at least every other year.

Earlier crops with higher yields are obtained by starting seed tubers into growth before planting, this process is known as 'chitting'. It is important that chitting is done in good light to produce short, tough shoots. Shoots produced in the dark are long, white, weak and useless. Seed potatoes for early production are purchased in late Autumn. Small tubers, i.e. weighing around 15 g (oz) give the best value for money and produce the best crops. The traditional practice of cutting large seed tubers longitudinally in half is not recommended. The tubers are placed in a single layer in trays with their rose end upwards.

The trays are kept in good light at temperatures no lower than 10°C (50°F) until March. When chitting begins, the numbers of shoots per tuber are reduced to two or three by rubbing off the smaller ones. The chitted tubers are hardened off at lower temperatures for a week or so before planting. Maincrop potatoes also benefit from chitting.

These are chitted in the light, following storage at low temperatures but above freezing.

Planting

In most districts potatoes are planted during March and early April. Holes are dug with a trowel deep enough to allow 5cm (2in) of soil above the tuber. A single tuber is dropped into each hole with shoots uppermost. The hole is then filled with soil.

Spacing

Early potatoes are planted in rows 60cm (2ft) apart with 23cm (9in) between the tubers. If the tubers are large the spacing is increased to 30cm(12in). Maincrop potatoes are planted in rows 75cm (2ft 6in) apart with 40cm (15in) between the tubers.

Fertilising

Potatoes are top dressed with 10% nitrogen fertiliser at the rate of 150g per sq m (4oz sq yd) for earlies and 190g per sq m (6oz per sq yd)

for maincrop. The top dressing is usually applied just before earthing up.

Earthing Up

When frost is likely the emerging shoots are covered with soil by 'earthing up'. A draw hoe is used to pull soil from between the rows over the potatoes, transforming a flat area into a ridged one. The ridges not only protect the foliage from frost they also exclude light that would turn the developing tubers green. Earthing up also destroys any weeds that are growing, further weeding is usually unnecessary as the potato haulm (stems + leaves) quickly gives a dense cover, excluding the light. By careful manipulation of spacing and stem population it is possible to grow potatoes on the flat, growing in ridges is easier and more reliable.

Watering

Earlies:
There is usually sufficient water in

the soil during April and early May to satisfy the needs of early potatoes. When the new tubers have reached the size of small marbles, (it is necessary to scratch gently into the soil to verify this stage of development) apply a single watering of 22 litres sq m (4gal per sq yd).

Maincrop:
When the plants begin to flower apply 27 litres per sq m (5gal per sq yd). In dry weather repeat every two weeks. If water is given after a prolonged dry period the tubers may split.

Harvest

Early potatoes are usually ready for lifting as soon as the plants have finished flowering. The tops of a single plant are held whilst a garden fork is inserted at a 45° angle entering the soil some 22cm (9in) from the plant. The fork is used as a lever to lift the plant at the same time as the tops are pulled up. The tubers are picked from the

Stages in harvesting potatoes

Grower's Timetable EARLY POTATOES	
Autumn	Dig and manure potato plot (no lime).
November	Place in a single layer of small tubers rose end up in a trays, store in a warm light place.
February	Move tray of tubers to a cooler but frost free light place to harden.
Early March	Rake the soil to a coarse tilth.
	Plant tubers with 5cm (2in) of soil above them in rows 60cm (2ft) apart and 23cm (9in) between the tubers.
April/May	Draw soil over the shoots as they emerge – especially in frosty weather.
	Top dress with 150 g per square metre (4 oz sq yd) with 10% nitrogen. Earth up into ridges.
June	Water in dry weather. Harvest as required.
	As soon as the ground is cleared plant another crop.

Grower's Timetable – MAINCROP POTATOES	
Autumn	Dig in a large quantity of manure or compost into the soil (no lime).
Late March/ early April	Rake to a coarse tilth.
	Plant tubers with 5cm (2in) of soil above them in rows 75cm (2ft 6in) apart and 40cm (15in) between the tubers.
May	Protect emerging shoots from frost by drawing soil over them.
	Top dress with 190g (5oz per sq yd) of 10% nitrogen fertiliser. Earth up into ridges.
June/September	If blight is forecast spray with fungicide (page 56).
	Water in dry weather.
September/October	When tops die down harvest, dry and store in paper sacks.

root and collected from the soil. The soil is then forked over to search for any stray tubers. It is important to remove every tuber to prevent disease being carried into the following season. Freshly harvested potatoes are subject to physical damage and should be handled as gently as eggs. Maincrop potatoes are not lifted until the tops have died down. At this stage the skins will be firm and the tubers will keep in store. Maincrop tubers are forked out and left on the surface for an hour or so to dry before picking.

Storing

After drying, maincrop potatoes are sorted and any which are damaged or imperfect are removed for immediate use. The perfect tubers are put into thick brown paper sacks and stored in a cold but frost free building. The twin walled paper sacks 'breath' and keep an ideal storage humidity around the tubers, they also exclude the light. Potatoes are alive and therefore are respiring and producing water all the time, if stored in plastic bag they soon become wet and begin to deteriorate.

Star Varieties

Early:

Maris Bard
Very early.

Pentland Javelin
A little later but a good cropper.

Maincrop:

Cara
Excellent flavour - therefore liable to slug damage!

Maris Piper
High yielding but susceptible to drought, attractive tubers.

Cooking

After lifting, the sugars in new potatoes begins to convert to starch. It is important therefore to lift new potatoes only as required. Do not scrape the tubers - just wash them, put into a saucepan and just cover with lightly salted water. Add a sprig of fresh mint, put the lid on and bring to the boil, simmer gently until the largest tuber is tender (test with a fine skewer). Drain and serve, or allow to cool and serve with salad.

With maincrop potatoes it is better to peel them after cooking. If potatoes are peeled before cooking they should be peeled as thinly as possible in order to retain the nutrients.

Large potatoes are excellent when baked in a microwave oven - my children say that they are even better when chipped and deep fried!

PUMPKINS & SQUASHES

Curcubita maxima, C. argyrosperma, C. moschata & C. pepo.

Four different species of annual plants are grown as pumpkins or squashes. In addition to this there are many different types of each species. The Royal Horticultural Society list over eighty varieties and that is not a complete list. The distinction between pumpkins and squashes is very loose, the word 'pumpkin' usually applies to the types which have the coarse orange flesh used for pumpkin pie and the word 'squash' refers to the white fleshed, milder tasting types. To add to the confusion, squashes are further divided into winter and summer types. Whatever we call them, they are fun to grow and, with some recipes they can be delicious to eat.

Varieties of these species with small fruits are grown for ornamental purposes and are usually referred to as 'ornamental gourds'.

Pumpkins and squashes are grown in exactly the same way as marrows. For details turn to page 84.

Star Varieties

For giant 'halloween' pumpkins:

Hundredweight
Oval to round in shape, fine textured orange flesh. (trailing plant)

Squashes

Butternut
Pear shaped fruits which weigh up to 1kg (2lb), one of the best types for use as a vegetable (trailing plant).

Sweet Mama
Produces a lot of small green fruits with a sweet flavour (bush plant).

Tapping a squash to test for ripeness

Pumpkin soup served in the hollowed out pumpkin stays hot and makes a good talking point for a dinner party

RADICCHIO
Cichorium intybus

Although this crop is usually grown in a similar way to lettuce it is not a lettuce – it is a chicory (the Italian word for chicory is radicchio). It is a fairly new crop in the UK which is becoming increasingly popular. It is very easy to grow and deserves a place in every vegetable (or flower!) garden.

Radicchio's sharp flavour and attractive colour make it an ideal ingredient in mixed salads. It is also most useful as a garnish, with some varieties having bright red heads whilst others can be blanched to an attractive pink/white. All are cut and come again crops.

Soil
Any soil with plenty of organic matter and a pH between 5.5 and 7.0 will support a crop of radiccio.

Sowing and Planting
As with most crops radicchio plants can be raised inside and transplanted outside later. This crop is quite hardy and good results are usually obtained by direct sowing and thinning. The soil is raked to a fine tilth and seeds are sown in drills 12mm (½in) deep.

Spacing
Rows 35cm (14in) apart with 25cm (10in) between the plants is ideal for most varieties. The variety Cesare is rather large and needs 40cm(16in) between rows and plants.

Fertilising
A top dressing of 100g per sq m (3oz per sq yd) of 10% nitrogen fertiliser is applied a week or so after the final thinning. For transplanted crops the fertiliser is worked into the bed before planting.

Watering
Frequent watering of up to 15 litres per sq m (3gal per sq yd) each week during the early stages of growth. Radicchio forms a deep tap root and watering can be reduced once the plants are well established.

Harvest
Radicchio plants can be harvested by cutting off at ground level in a similar way to lettuce; alternatively individual leaves may be taken. Either way the crop will regrow.

Star Variety

Palla Rossa
Matures in September from a June sowing, heart of deep red with fine white veins.

Giulio
An early variety sown in May, harvest in July.

Cooking
Although radicchio is most often used as a garnish or in salads, it can be lightly boiled and used as a vegetable. It is also a useful addition to a stirfry.

Radicchio photographed in November is a hardier plant than lettuce

---

Grower's Timetable – RADICCHIO
Radicchio is a useful catch-crop and a useful crop can be obtained by sowing after early potatoes, spring cabbage or salad crops.

April	Work the soil to a fine tilth and sow an early variety in rows 35cm (14in) apart.
May	Thin seedlings to 25cm (10in) apart.
	Top dress with 100g per sq m (3oz per sq yd) of 10% nitrogen fertiliser.
	Control weeds.
	Water if necessary.
July	Harvest as required
	Make a second sowing of a late variety
August	Thin seedlings to 25cm (10in) apart.
	Control weeds.
October	Harvest as required.

NB Some radicchio roots will force inside in a similar way to whitloof chicory – see page 82.

RADISH
Raphanus sativus

Originating in the Eastern Mediterranean, this annual plant is grown for its edible taproot. Radishes were cultivated in Egypt over 2,000 years ago and are now grown throughout the world. The radish is a hardy plant that matures very quickly, there are many shapes and sizes, some which mature in winter and some which mature in summer. Although radishes can be grown all the year round, production in high summer can be difficult as the plants may run to seed before any taproot is formed.

Soil
Light soils are best for growing radish, but they need to be rich and well drained. Any pH value between 5.5 and 7.0 is satisfactory. Although it is not a brassica the radish is susceptible to the brassica pests and diseases; radish should therefore be grown in the same rotation as the brassicas.

Radish damaged by slugs

Sowing
Seeds are sown in drills 2cm (1in) deep. Older radishes become tough and hot to the taste; regular sowings of small amounts are made to ensure a continuous supply of young roots.

Spacing
Rows need to be 15cm (6in) apart and seeds must be sown thinly. Thickly sown radishes produce lots of leaves but the roots are thin and useless. If soil conditions are good, one seed every centimetre (about three to the inch) will produce the best yield in the shortest time. Winter radishes are larger and require more space. Rows of winter radish are spaced 20cm (8in) apart with 10cm (4in) between the plants.

Fertilising
Radishes mature very quickly and require all their nutrients at a very early stage of growth. 25g per sq m (1oz per sq yd) of 10% nitrogen fertiliser raked into the seed bed is all that is required.

Watering
Too much water produces lush leaves and poor roots. Water is applied to the bottom of the drill before sowing to aid germination. In dry weather watering is restricted to once each week when 11 litres per sq m (2gal per sq yd) is applied along the rows.

Harvest
Roots of summer radish are harvested as soon as they reach an edible size, otherwise they become hot and woody. If the largest roots are slightly rotated between finger and thumb as they are pulled, the smaller ones alongside will remain undisturbed and can be left to grow. Some varieties of winter radish are long and must be harvested with a garden fork. Unlike summer radish, winter radish stand in good condition for a long time and can be left in the ground until required.

Star Varieties

Summer varieties:
Summer Crunch
Cylinder shape, deep pink with a white tip, crisp and sweet.

Cherry Belle
Scarlet globe shape roots with crisp white flesh.

Winter variety:
China Rose
Large, stump ended roots with pink skin and white flesh.

Grower's timetable – RADISH	
March	Sowings can be made under cloches.
April through to late July	Sow summer varieties every three weeks. Mix two varieties to extend harvest period. Sow 2cm (1 n) deep, one seed per centimetre, two or three seeds per inch in rows 15cm (6in) apart. Control weeds and harvest as soon as the roots are large enough to eat. Early June Sow a winter variety for Autumn use, rows 20cm (8in) apart with 10cm (4in) between the plants.
Late July	Make a second sowing of a winter variety for winter use.
December	In cold districts, cover with straw or cloches for frost protection.

RHUBARB
Rheum x cultorum
Rhubarb is a hybrid from the East which first appeared in Europe during the eighteenth century. Similar species were grown in China 5,000 years ago and used as a laxative. Rhubarb leaves contain oxalic acid which is very poisonous and should on no account be eaten. The petioles (leaf stalks) are thick and fleshy, they are used in pies and preserves in a similar way to fruit. Rhubarb is a perennial which requires a permanent place in the garden; it is usually sited in an odd corner for convenience rather than being given the best available growing conditions. A rhubarb bed will remain productive for 15 years or more.

Soil
Most moisture retentive soils will grow rhubarb. Good drainage is important as the thick roots do not withstand water-logging for any length of time. Rhubarb grows in soils with a pH as low as 4.5 but a higher pH (6.5) produces better growth.

Thorough soil preparation is essential, the area must be deeply worked and a large amount of organic matter is mixed in together with a liberal amount of bonemeal.

Sowing and Planting
Rhubarb is easily grown from seed. Seeds can be sown directly into the rhubarb bed; it is very much better to raise them in pots in a cold frame one year and plant out in early spring the next. Growing from seed is generally not recommended; however the author has done it many times with considerable success.

The most usual method of establishing a rhubarb bed is to purchase crowns, i e a piece of root with a dormant bud on top. These are planted vertically with the bud protruding just above the soil.

Spacing

Rhubarb leaves are very large and require a lot of space. The ideal distance between rhubarb plants is 1m (39in) but where space is limited a distance of 90cm (35in) may be used.

Fertilising

The best way to keep a rhubarb bed supplied with nutrients is to apply a good dressing of rotted manure or compost in late autumn. If this is not available, complete fertiliser should be applied in early spring. Growmore, analysis 7 : 7 : 7, applied at the rate of 100g per sq m (4oz per sq yd) is suitable, if another type is used the amount is adjusted according to its analysis.

Watering

Rhubarb has a high water requirement especially in spring and early summer. It is deep rooted and watering is usually unnecessary. If the rainfall is very low in spring, water applied each week at the rate of 11 litres per sq m (2gal per sq yd) will enhance yield.

Forcing and Blanching.

Rhubarb can be induced to grow very early in the year by covering the crowns with straw and inverting an opaque cover over the top; a black painted oil drum is ideal. The additional warmth starts early growth and the absence of light causes the stems to elongate. In order to maintain the vigour of the crowns, a different area of the bed should be forced each year.

A very early indoor crop can be grown by digging crowns, complete with the roots in early winter. These are left lying on the surface, after two or three severe frosts they are potted (or boxed) up in peat or soil and kept in the dark at temperatures between 7° & 16°C (45° - 65°F). It is important that the plants are kept within this temperature range as too cold they will not grow and too warm the shoots will be very spindly. After harvest the roots are discarded.

Harvesting

Young stems with crinkled leaves are selected, these must not be cut but grasped near to the bottom and pulled up. The leaves are cut off and must not be eaten. It is important that three or four large leaves remain on each plant as they provide the materials for growth. Harvesting continues from early spring until June. After this the bed must be left to recover and build up reserves for the following year's harvest.

Rhubarb seedlings

Grower's Timetable – RHUBARB

Establishing a bed:
from seeds

April	Sow seeds in a tray of compost and keep in a cold greenhouse or garden frame. Prick out into individual 7cm (3in) pots. Pot on up to 22cm pots.
Late summer	Select an area which is completely free of perennial weeds. Note: glyphosate (sold as 'Roundup') will clear perennial weeds but it must be applied whilst they are actively growing - see page 43. Thoroughly prepare the area by deep digging, adding a lot of decaying organic matter and 200g per sq m (8oz per sq yd) of bonemeal.
Autumn or early Spring	Plant home grown plants **OR** purchased crowns with the buds just above soil level. Allow 1m (39in) between plants.
All summer	Water if necessary. Control weeds.
The following year.	Do not harvest any stalks - wait until the year after. Control weeds. Remove any flower shoots as soon as they appear.

Maintaining an established bed.

February	Cover part of the bed with straw and an opaque drum to produce early stems.
March - June	Harvest as required, always leave four leaves on each plant. Control weeds - there are unlikely to be any as the rhubarb leaves shade them out.
Late Autumn	Give a mulch of well rotted manure or compost.

Star Varieties

From seed:
Glaskins
Quick growing, red sticks of good length and quality.

From Crowns:
Timperley Early
Suitable for forcing.

Painted Lady grown on a wigwam

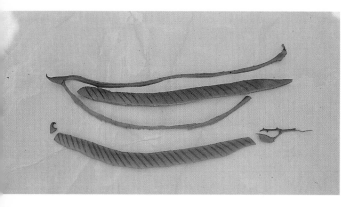

Preparing runner beans for the kitchen. The old variety on top needs trimming all the way round. The stringless variety below only needs topping and tailing

Victoria
A good mid-season type with excellent flavour.

Cooking
Rhubarb should not be cooked in an aluminum pan as the acids it contains may dissolve a slight amount of the metal. Peel the stalks and cut into 3cm (1in) lengths.

RUNNER BEANS
Phaseolus coccineus
The runner bean is a native of Mexico where it still grows in the wild. This perennial plant is usually grown as an annual. An early, but poor crop of runner beans can be obtained by storing the underground parts in frost free conditions throughout the winter, and planting the following spring

When sliced and boiled the thick fleshy pods are a very succulent vegetable – especially if they are young and freshly picked. The runner bean is one of the most popular vegetables in this country – and also one of the least hardy.

Soil
Thorough soil preparation is essential for a successful crop of runner beans. Mature plants have a very large leaf area and consequently require large amounts of water. This is met in part by deep cultivations and the addition of large amounts of well rotted manure or compost. Ideally the pH should be around 6.5. In windy areas the most

sheltered site should be used. The traditional method of opening a two-spit deep trench, putting organic matter into the bottom and then back filling, is not recommended. Much better results are obtained by mixing the organic matter with the soil to a depth of two spits.

Support
The supporting structures are best erected before the seeds are sown. A double row of eight foot canes pushed firmly into the ground, crossed over and tied to a horizontal cane makes a firm structure. Pyramids of eight canes may also be used, the canes equally spaced around a circle diameter 120cm (4ft) and pushed vertically into the ground. The tops of the canes are then pulled together and firmly tied with string.

Other methods of support include large mesh nets and individual vertical strings. Whatever method is used a firm anchorage is essential – especially in windy areas. Runner beans can also be grown along the ground. This method takes a lot of space and the crop is subject to rain splashing and slug attack.

Spacing
For good yields canes are placed 30cm (1ft) apart along the row with the rows 60cm (2ft) apart. If more than one double row is grown, the path between two rows is 90cm (3ft) wide. These spacings allow for two plants to be grown on each cane. Higher yields are obtained by spacing canes 15cm (6in) apart and

Place the cut stalks in a pan, pour boiling water over them, bring back to the boil and drain. This considerably reduces the acid. Add sugar to the blanched stalks and poach gently until tender. Caution! rhubarb cooks quickly and is easily overdone.

growing one plant on each cane.

Sowing
Seeds are sown in mid May. Three seeds are pushed into the soil around each cane to a depth of 5cm (2in). If three seedlings appear at a single station the weakest one is removed.

Earlier crops are obtained by raising plants in a greenhouse and planting out the first week of June (or when the risk of frost has passed). Seeds are sown individually in 7cm (3in) pots or deep root trainers, using a good multipurpose compost. It is essential that these plants are thoroughly hardened off (see Glossary) before planting out. A protection of fleece tied along the row for the first 2 weeks helps the plants to establish and grow away quickly. Where slugs are likely to damage the young plants, pellets or beer traps should be used.

Raising several plants in one pot is not recommended, the root disturbance on planting out gives an unnecessary check to growth.

Fertilising
Runner beans have bacteria associated with their roots which produce nitrates from the soil air. In properly prepared, well managed soil additional fertiliser is not required. A foliar feed of Phostrogen or Miraclegro may be helpful if plants are looking pale or chlorotic.

Watering
Runner beans require copious amounts of water especially at

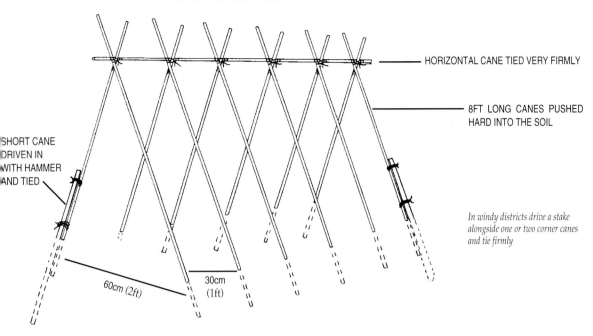

HORIZONTAL CANE TIED VERY FIRMLY

8FT LONG CANES PUSHED HARD INTO THE SOIL

SHORT CANE DRIVEN IN WITH HAMMER AND TIED

In windy districts drive a stake alongside one or two corner canes and tie firmly

60cm (2ft)

30cm (1ft)

flowering and fruiting time. In dry weather watering begins when the first flowers appear. 22 litres per sq m (4gal per sq yd) are given each week when there is no rainfall. Watering is of course reduced according to the amount of rainfall. The water is applied directly to the soil and not sprayed onto the flowers. Watering is continued throughout the fruiting period.

Harvesting

The yield obtained from a row of runner beans is increased by regular harvesting. The pods are picked when fully grown but before the beans inside begin to swell. Two hands are used, one to hold the stem and the other to pull off the beans. Picking is done every 3 days and any pods which were missed at a previous picking are picked and discarded. If seed is to be saved for the following year, it is best to leave two plants at the end of a row to provide these rather than leave the odd pod which has been missed.

If a row is to be left unattended for a week all the developing pods are removed, otherwise the seeds will begin to mature and the plants will stop flowering as a result.

Pollination

In order for runner beans to be set the flowers must be pollinated, any which are not are aborted. The flower trumpet is an unusual spiral shape and only bees with long tongues can obtain the nectar and hence pollinate the flower. In some seasons a short tongued bee will obtain nectar by biting a hole at the base of the flower. Other types of bee also make use of this hole and the flowers remain unpollinated. If an otherwise healthy row of beans suddenly stops production the bees should be observed to see if this is the cause. Nothing can be done to prevent this, fortunately the bees which bite the holes are only present for 2 or 3 weeks, once they go, pollination recommences.

Star Varieties

Desiree
A very high yielding, stringless variety. White flowers.

Red Knight
A stringless variety with red flowers.

Dwarf varieties are available but these have the disadvantage of the

Grower's Timetable – RUNNER BEANS	
Autumn	Prepare the soil.
Mid April	Sow seeds in the greenhouse.
Early May	Erect the supports.
Mid May	Sow seeds by each support.
Early June	Plant out **hardened off** plants or thin seedlings to one or two per support. Take precautions against slugs.
July - September	Water as required - most important! Harvest at least every third day.

pods being in contact with the soil.

* In some areas it is traditional to save runner bean seed from one year to the next, the author's mother saved her own seeds for over 40 years. The author does not follow her example as he would lose the benefits of the modern hybrids. On no account should seeds from hybrid varieties be saved.

Cooking
Runner beans are better boiled rather than steamed. Mature pods of non-stringless varieties are trimmed all the way round to remove the strings. Stringless varieties are just topped and tailed. Pods are sliced obliquely before being dropped into boiling **slightly** salted water. They are then boiled gently until **just** tender.

Freezing
The beans are prepared as for cooking and blanched for one minute. After draining they are cooled in cold water, the slices are then spread on a metal tray and frozen. Once frozen the beans are transferred to a plastic box for convenient storage and use. Many say that frozen runners are just a good as fresh ones, those who prefer their vegetables crisp are unlikely to agree.

Runner bean canes do not have to cross over at the top

Salsify

SALSIFY & SCORZONERA
Tragopogon porrifolius and Scorzonera hispanica
These two closely related undemanding plants are extremely easy to grow and are unaffected by most pests and diseases. The large taproots are edible and have a delicate taste although unworthy of the name 'vegetable oyster'. The name scorzonera comes from the word 'scorpion' as a related plant was used in Spain to cure snake bites. Salsify has white roots and scorzonera has black roots. When the black peel of scorzonera is removed, the inside is a pure white which quickly discolours. The yield of both salsify and scorzonera is poor when compared with other root vegetables.

Soil
Most soils are suitable providing they are free of fresh manure and have a pH in excess of 6.5.

Sowing
Seeds are large enough to handle individually and can be placed where the plants are intended to grow. Two seeds are sown at each station at a depth of 2cm (1in).

Spacing
Rows 30cm (12in) apart with plants 20cm (8in) apart gives an ideal population.

Fertilising
A single top dressing in early June of 10% nitrogen fertiliser applied at the rate of 70g per sq m (2oz per sq yd) is all that is required.

Watering
These plants are very deep rooted and once established require no watering.

Harvest
Salsify and scorzonera are very hardy and can be left in the ground throughout the winter. The plants are dug up with a fork as required; care is needed as the roots are deep and easily broken.

Star Variety

Sandwich Island
Salsify with a smooth texture.

Cooking
Scrape the roots and rewash them. Cut into 5cm (2in) lengths. Steam until tender, take care not to overcook.

Grower's Timetable – SALSIFY & SCORZONERA	
April	Sow seeds in pairs 20cm (8in) apart in rows 30cm (12in) apart.
May	Remove weakest seedling from each pair.
June to September	Apply a top dressing of 10% nitrogen at the rate of 70g per sq m (2oz per sq yd). Keep weed free by hand and mulching. (roots bleed if damaged by a hoe).
Winter	Harvest as required.

SCORZONERA
see Salsify

SHALLOT
Allium cepa aggregatum
This plant originated in Asia where it has been cultivated for thousands of years for its edible leaves and bulb. It is a very hardy perennial which can withstand extremes of temperatures, both hot and cold. The shallot is used either for pickling or as an onion substitute. Shallots keep longer and mature earlier than onions, this makes them particularly useful in early summer when there may be a gap in the onion supply.

The Bulbs
Shallots are grown from bulbs. A single bulb produces a number of offsets which develop into full grown bulbs. A bulb planted in spring will have developed into ten or more by the summer, Firm

bulbs weighing around 10g (⅓oz) are selected for high yields.

Many gardeners save their own bulbs for planting the following year. This is both cheap and effective, however there is a possibility that virus diseases will begin to build up. If several plants appear to be stunted new stock should be purchased from a reputable supplier.

Soil

Shallots are very easy to grow, especially in light fertile soils, heavy clay soils are less suitable. A pH between 6 and 7 is ideal. The best results are obtained in firm ground, to achieve this the soil is dug and manured in autumn and left to settle during winter.

Planting

The shallot is usually the first vegetable to be planted, in some areas this may be as early as February. Planting is done on a dry day in early spring, the soil is raked to break up any large lumps and to leave a level surface. Individual bulbs are pushed into the soil and left with just the tips showing above the surface. On heavy soils damage to the bulbs is avoided by drawing a drill or making planting holes with a trowel. In some gardens the birds pull them up, this is prevented by hiding the tip with a little soil. By the time this has been washed off by rain the shallots will have rooted.

Spacing

The bulbs are planted at 10cm (4in) intervals in rows 30cm (12in) apart. A better spacing, for use on raised beds, is 15 x 20cm (6 x 8in).

Watering

If the spring is exceptionally dry some watering may be necessary to establish the plants, after this time shallots are best left un-watered.

Harvesting

When the leaves begin to die back in July and the bulbs are ready for harvesting. They are eased out of the ground with a fork and left on the surface for a week or so to ripen. When quite dry they are taken indoors for use or storage.

Storing

If firm, disease free shallots are kept dry with **good air circulation** they will remain in excellent condition until the following summer. Thin layers of bulbs on slatted trays is the best method, hanging up in nets and even ladies stockings is often recommended. If too many shallots are put into a standard onion net, the bulbs in the middle will become wet and deteriorate.

Star Varieties

Pikant

Strong flavour, a good keeper and very bolt resistant.

Cooking

Although some recipes specify shallots, they are more often used used in the kitchen as a substitute for onions.

Shallots ready for harvest

Grower's Timetable – SHALLOTS	
Autumn	Dig manure or compost into soil.
March	Rake to a medium tilth Plant bulbs 10cm (4in) apart along rows 30cm (12in) apart, leave the tip of the bulb just showing.
April - June	Keep weed free by hand or **shallow** hoeing.
July	Lift, dry and store.

SPINACH

Spinacia oleracea

Several different plants are eaten as spinach; the true spinach is an annual that originated in Central Asia. It is a cool season crop which gives the best results in spring and late autumn. Summer sowings may run to seed before a crop of leaves have developed. There are two forms, one with round seeds which is spring sown and harvested throughout the summer and the other with prickly seeds, is autumn sown and withstands winter conditions.

Successional sowings of summer spinach are often recommended to provide spinach throughout the summer. An easier method of producing spinach in high summer is to grow spinach beet or New Zealand spinach.

Spinach beet (sometimes called 'perpetual spinach') is a form of beetroot which is grown for its edible leaves. If not sown too early (ie before mid May) it will produce leaves throughout the summer before bolting.

New Zealand spinach is a tender, sprawling perennial. The seeds are rather difficult to germinate and this plant is best raised in pots for planting out in early June with plenty of space – at least 60cm (24in) between the plants.

Soil

Spinach has a high water requirement and performs best on soil which is both water retentive and free draining. It does not tolerate acid soils and a pH of 7.0 or even higher should be aimed for.

A lot of spinach has to be harvested as it boils down to a small amount when cooked

Sowing

Spinach does not transplant and is grown from seeds sown in situ. A one gallon bucket, loosely filled with spinach leaves, becomes just two tablespoons of cooked vegetable. A reasonable area of spinach should therefore be sown; 4m (4yds) per person should be allowed. A fine tilth is required to obtain an even sowing depth of 1cm (½in).

Spacing

Spinach plants with sufficient space are less likely to bolt than those which are closely packed. Rows need to be 30cm (12in) apart and the seedlings thinned to 15 cm (6 in) along the row.

Fertilising

Spinach responds well to nitrogen fertiliser and up to 170g per sq m (6oz per sq yd) of 10% nitrogen fertiliser can be used. One third of this can be raked into the seed bed and the rest applied as a top dressing a week or so after thinning out.

Watering

Frequent watering is necessary for high quality, rapid growth and maximum yield. Up to 22 litres per sq m (4gal per sq yd) can be applied each week during periods of hot, dry weather.

Harvest

If left too long the large leaves tend to become stringy. To prevent this, either harvest regularly or leave the old leaves on the plants and harvest the young ones. Leaves can be picked individually or the whole plant can be cut off 5cm (2in) above the ground. Either way a new crop will grow if conditions are favourable.

Star Variety

Atlanta
A high yielding frost resistant strain with thick, dark green leaves.

Cooking

Remove and discard the stems. Wash well. Place in a pan with 2cm (1in) of boiling water in the bottom. Turn with a plastic spoon until all the leaves are cooked (about 3 minutes). Transfer to a colander, squeeze out as much water as possible with the back of the spoon and serve.

Grower's Timetable – SPINACH	
February	Cover an area with cloche.
March	Sow under cloche.
April	Make a second sowing in open ground, 1cm (½in) deep in rows 30cm (12in) apart . Thin seedlings to 15cm (6in) apart along the row as soon as they are large enough to handle.
May	Control weeds. Top dress with 100g per sq m (4 oz per sq yd) of 10% nitrogen fertiliser. Harvest leaves as required.
June	Water in dry weather. Control weeds. Harvest.
July and August	Water/ control weeds and harvest. Sow for Autumn use.
September	Make a final sowing, these plants will stand the winter and crop in April.
October and November	Harvest

SPROUTING BROCCOLI
see Cauliflower

SQUASHES
see Pumpkin

SUGAR SNAPS
see Peas

SWEDES
Brassica napus
The Swedish turnip, commonly called a swede, is a hardy biennial that differs from other turnips in several ways. It is larger, hardier, stores better, has a milder taste and takes longer to grow.

Soil
Almost any soil will produce a crop of swedes providing the pH is not too low. This should be between 5.5 and 6.5. Swedes are brassicas and must be grown in the same plot as cabbages in the rotation.

Sowing
Flea beetles have a strong preference for swede seedlings and will destroy the crop unless precautions are taken; delaying sowing until June or covering with fleece

are as effective as insecticides in the control of this pest.

Swedes are direct sown and thinned out to the required final distance. As the seeds are small, a fine tilth is needed in order to achieve an equal sowing depth of 2.0 to 2.5cm (½ to 1 in). If the soil is dry the bottom of the drill is watered before sowing.

Spacing

Rows are spaced 30cm apart and the seedlings are thinned to 22cm (9in) apart along the row.

Fertilising

A top dressing of 70g per sq m (2oz per sq yd) of 10% nitrogen is applied two weeks after thinning out.

Watering

A lot of water produces large swedes with a rather poor flavour, some water may be needed however to prevent the soil from drying out. The recommended amount is 11 litres per square metre (2gal per sq yd) applied along the row during the early stages of growth.

Harvest

The roots are simply pulled up as required and the tops and roots trimmed with a sharp knife. In all but the mildest districts swedes deteriorate progressively throughout the winter. Swedes store well providing they have a low temperature and a high humidity. **Undamaged** swedes can be stored in slatted wooden boxes with sand added to each layer to prevent them from touching. Swedes intended for storing should have the leaves twisted off and the roots left on.

Star Variety

Marian
Light purple skin with good sized spherical roots, some resistance to powdery mildew and clubroot disease (sometimes called 'finger and toe' disease).

Cooking

Prepare by peeling and cutting into cubes. If only part of a root is used the remainder will keep in a fridge providing the cut part is protected by clingfilm.

Swedes are used in casseroles and stews. They make an excellent vegetable when steamed, mashed with butter and then baked in the oven for 15 minutes.

Swede – Marian

Grower's Timetable – SWEDE	
Early June	Sow seeds thinly in the brassica plot in rows 30cm (1ft) apart.
July	Thin out to leave single plants 22cm (9in) apart.
	Control weeds.
	In dry weather water and watch for powdery mildew.
	Spray systemic fungicide if necessary.
August/September	Control weed.
October/December	Harvest as required.
January	Lift and store (not in mild areas).

The cob on the right shows the effect of poor pollination

SWEETCORN
Zea mays

Sweetcorn is a type of maize. Maize has been cultivated in South America for over 5,000 years and is now the most widely grown cereal in tropical and warmer areas of the world. The variety of maize suitable for growing as sweetcorn in Britain is a comparative recent introduction and it is now possible to grow a successful crop in most parts of the country.

Soil

When growing sweetcorn soil temperature is of extreme importance – it must be warm, and certainly above 10°C (50°F). Most soils with a pH between 5.5 and 7 will support a crop of maize providing there is good light and some shelter from north and east winds where these are troublesome.

Sowing

In warm areas and where the ground has been pre-warmed with plastic sheeting sowings can be made directly into the soil. Seeds are sown individually at a depth of 5cm (2in). In other areas it is better to use transplants. To avoid transplanting check, and the subsequent yield reduction each plant should be grown in its own container and carefully hardened off.

Raising sweetcorn plants:
1. Fill a block of large root trainers with seed compost.

2. Sow when the cherry trees are in full blossom.

3. Push one seed into each section to a depth of 5cm (2in).

4. Water well and place on the staging.

5. Three or four weeks after germination give a light feed with a high nitrogen fertiliser.

6. As soon as the risks of frost are over, harden off and plant outside.

Pollination and Spacing
Sweetcorn is pollinated by wind and gravity, the male flowers stand high above the top of the plants and shed copious amounts

of pollen. The female flower is an immature cob with a thin tube leading from each grain and hanging from the end forming the 'silk'. In order for all the seeds to develop each strand of silk must receive its own pollen grain. Good pollination is therefore essential and to achieve this, sweetcorn is not grown in rows but in a square block. Blocks with sixteen or more plants spaced 35cm (14in) apart have a good chance of complete pollination.

Fertilising

Direct sown plants are top dressed with 120g per sq m (3oz per sq yd) of 10% nitrogen fertiliser. A similar amount is applied to the plant bed just before transplanting.

Watering

Once the plants are established, watering is not normally necessary. However a better crop is obtained by giving 22 litres per sq m (4gal per sq yd) once the tassel (male flower) begins to form at the top. The same amount of water is given once or twice (depending

Male flower (above) and female flower (below)

upon rainfall) during cob swelling. Watering increases the cob size and improves the quality.

Harvest

After pollination the silks begin to turn brown, this is an indication that the cob is maturing. The leaves covering the cob are carefully peeled away to reveal a small section of seeds, if these are plump, soft and yellow the cob is ready for harvest. Cobs left beyond this stage begin to harden and lose their sweetness. The cob is harvested by bending downwards until it snaps off. Plants usually produce two cobs, the uppermost prime cob matures a little before the lower one which is usually smaller and somewhat inferior.

After harvesting the sugars in the seeds begin to turn to starch, the cobs should therefore be eaten or frozen as soon as possible after harvest.

Star Varieties

Only one variety should be grown at a time as cross pollination be-

tween varieties is likely to spoil the flavour.

Tasty Sweet

An F1 Hybrid with excellent taste and suitable for growing in all areas.

Rosella

An F1 Hybrid with large cobs, good cold tolerance.

Cooking

Peel the cobs and trim the ends square. Microwave for 15 minutes on high setting. Fix a sweetcorn holder into each end, add a little butter and serve at once. Alternatively the seeds can be stripped from the cob with a sharp knife and cooked as a vegetable or served in salad.

Freezing

Peel the cobs and trim the ends square. Blanch in boiling water for one minute, cool quickly and freeze.

Grower's Timetable – SWEETCORN

In warm frost free areas:

April	Cover the soil with clear plastic.
End of May	Sow seeds in a square block, two per station 35cm (14in) apart each way.
June	Pull out weakest seedling from any doubles.
	Top dress with 120g per sq m (3oz per sq yd) of 10% Nitrogen fertiliser.
	Control weeds.
July/August	Harvest as soon as ready.

In cooler areas where frosts may occur up to first week in June:

Early May	Sow seeds individually in pots or root trainers in a greenhouse.
Early June	Harden off.
Mid June	Rake into soil bed 120g per sq m (3oz per sq yd) of 10% Nitrogen fertiliser.
	Transplant in a square block 35cm (14in) between the plants each way.
	Control weeds.
July/August	Harvest as soon as ready.

TOMATOES

Lycopersicon lycopersicum

The wild tomato plant grows in Equador and Peru and was domesticated in Mexico before being transported to Europe during the sixteenth century. The large red fruits are edible but all other parts of the plant are poisonous. Although tomatoes are usually grown in greenhouses, they crop well outside in all but the coldest districts.

Soil

Any well drained and moisture retentive soil will support a crop of

tomatoes. A pH level of between 5.5 and 7.0 is suitable. A complete fertiliser should be raked into the soil before planting. (Growmore at the rate of 100g per sq m (3oz per sq yd). The tomato is closely related to the potato and they occupy the same bed in rotation systems.

Sowing and Planting.

The season is too short to produce tomatoes from seeds sown in situ. Outdoor tomatoes are therefore always grown from plants. These can be raised from seeds sown in a heated propagator at the beginning of March or they can be purchased. Care must be taken, when buying plants, that they are a variety which is suitable for outdoor culture. Plants are ready for planting when the first flowering truss is visible. The soil temperature should be at least 10°C (50°F) and there must be no risk of frost.

Spacing

A distance of 48 x 48cm (19 x 19in) between plants will give high yields with a good proportion of the fruit early in the season. Wider spacings give similar yields with a smaller proportion of the crop early in the season.

If tomatoes are grown on four foot wide raised beds they should be planted in rows of two, with each plant 38cm (15in) from the path and the rows 38cm (15in) apart.

Fertilising

If the plant leaves appear healthy and good trusses of fruit are forming; there are probably sufficient nutrients in the soil to meet requirements. If the leaves are pale or the veins a contrasting colour, a foliar feed of phostrogen or similar product can be given weekly.

Watering

Newly planted tomatoes require plenty of water until they become established. When fruiting begins the root activity slows, at this time the crop is very susceptible to water shortage. Ideally 11 litres per sq m (2gal per sq yd) should be given twice each week. More than this may increase the yield, but it will reduce the flavour. Too little water causes the fruits to have dark sunken areas at the end (a condition known as 'blossom end rot').

Support

Unlike greenhouse tomatoes the sideshoots on outdoor tomatoes are not removed, the plants are left to grow as bushes. No support is needed, small wooden boards or plastic, placed under the trusses prevents them from becoming soiled.

Harvest

Fruits are best removed before they become fully ripe. Picking is a two handed job, one hand to remove the fruit whilst the other supports the stem. The fruit should be picked complete with calyx and a short length of stalk.

Star varieties

Gardener's Delight
Small fruits with excellent flavour, good cropper.

Red Alert
Prolific and early cropping.

Outdoor tomatoes are not side shooted – they are grown as a bush

Grower's Timetable – TOMATOES	
Late March to mid April	Sow seeds in propagator (do not sow any earlier as light levels are too low) and raise plants in greenhouse, potting on as necessary.
June	Harden off plants or purchase them from a reliable supplier.
	Rake in 100g per sq m (3oz per sq yd) of complete fertiliser.
	Plant out when all risk of frost has gone, space 48cm (19in) each way.
July	Water as require.
	Control weeds.
	Place boards (or plastic) under the trusses.
August	Harvest fruit as soon as they begin to ripen.
September or October	Pick all remaining fruit before the first frost.
	Ripen inside or use in a green tomato recipe.

Varieties of Turnip

TURNIPS
Brassica rapa

Originating in southern Europe, turnips are grown mainly for their enlarged, fleshy roots although the young leaves can be eaten as greens. Turnips mature very rapidly producing a worthwhile crop in only 10 weeks.

Turnips are hardy, but not as hardy as swedes, an almost year round supply of root vegetables can be obtained by growing both of these crops.

Soil
Almost any soil will produce a crop of turnips providing the pH is not too low. This should be between 5.5 and 6.5. Turnips are brassicas and must be included with the cabbages, etcetera in the rotation.

Sowing and Planting.
Turnips are one of the few vegetables that are better not transplanted. The seeds are small and a fine tilth is necessary to ensure an even sowing depth of 2.0 to 2.5cm (¾ to 1 in). In dry weather, water is applied to the bottom of the drills before the seeds are put in.

Spacing
Rows are spaced 30cm (1ft) apart. When the seedlings are large enough to handle, the crop is thinned out allowing each turnip 10cm of row space (ie three plants per foot).

Fertilising
100g per sq m (3oz per sq yd) of 10% nitrogen fertiliser is raked into the soil before sowing. Further applications are unnecessary.

Watering
The earliest crops are unlikely to require any watering; later in the season the soil must not be allowed to become too dry, water during the early stages of growth. An application of 11 litres per sq m (2gal per sq yd) watered along the rows will give sufficient moisture. Watering turnips increases their size but reduces their flavour.

Bolting
Moist turnip seeds are very sensitive to cold. If a period of cold weather follows an early sowing the roots will not swell and the crop will bolt. March sowings should therefore be made under cloches which have been in position for 2 weeks. Sowings in the open ground should be delayed until April – the actual timing depending upon season and district.

Harvest
Successional sowings will produce roots from May until October and these may be left in the ground until December. Roots are pulled individually as they become large enough; the others being left to develop. Turnips are best when pulled young as early crops left in the ground for long periods become woody.

Star varieties

Golden ball
Small globe shaped roots with yellow skin and flesh.

Milan Purple Top
Very early, flat roots and white flesh.

Cooking
Turnips are widely used in stews and casseroles; they can also be served on their own.

Peel and cube the roots. Steam until tender. Either: add a knob of butter and a little pepper. Mash with a potato masher and serve. Or: Add a knob of butter to a pan and toss the cooked turnip cubes over fierce heat for a minute or two to glaze them.

Grower's Timetable – TURNIPS	
April	Sow in rows 30cm (12in) apart.
	Thin seedlings to 10cm (4in) apart.
May to early July	Control weed.
	Sow every three weeks.
	Thin seedlings as soon as they are large enough.
June/December	Harvest as required.
Note: Turnips will store but it is easier to use swedes instead of turnips during the winter.	

GLOSSARY

Aerobic	process which takes place in the presence of air
Anaerobic	process which takes place without air
Annual	plant that grows from seed, flowers and dies in one growing season.
Bastard trenching	digging to a depth of two spits by forking the bottom of a trench.
Biennial	plant which grows from seed, flowers the following year and then dies
Biological control	method of controlling pests by the introduction of an organism.
Brassica	member of the cabbage family
Cloche	low transparent structure to protect plants.
Complete fertiliser	a fertiliser which contains nitrates, phosphates and potash.
Compost	brown friable material produced from decayed plants.
Double digging	method of digging to a depth of two spits without bringing subsoil to the surface.
Drill	shallow trench in which seeds are sown.
f 1 hybrid	the first cross between two pure bred parents.
Fertile soil	a soil which produces a good crop.
Fertiliser	a substance which contains chemicals necessary for plant growth.
Fleece	a non-woven fabric which admits light; used to protect plants.
Foliar feeding	applying liquid fertiliser to a plant's leaves.
Frass	insect droppings.
Fungicide	a chemical substance which kills fungus.
Fungus	a large group of organisms which feed on organic matter while growing inside it.
Glyphosphate	a chemical which kills grass and other plants.
Half hardy	plant which can grow outside but is killed by frost.
Harden off	gradually acclimatise a greenhouse plant to outside conditions.
Herbicide	chemical substance which kills plants.
Horticultural fleece	a non-woven fabric which transmits light: used to protect plants.

Hydroponics	growing plants in a solution of nutrients instead of soil.
Intercropping	growing a row of plants between the rows of an unrelated crop.
Micro-nutrient	a chemical which plants require in very small amounts.
Mulch	a layer of material placed on the soil surface.
Multipurpose compost	material which is used in plant pots for sowing seeds or growing plants.
Pan	a hard layer of soil just below the depth of cultivation.
Perennial	a plant which lives for several years.
p H	the units by which the degree of acidity is measured.
Phosphate	an element which is essential for plant growth.
Planting stick	a straight piece of wood which enables plants to be planted in a straight line.
Potash	an element which is essential for plant growth.
Predator	an animal which eats other animals.
Rhizome	an underground stem.
Rotation	a system which ensures that no crop is grown in the same area more often than one year in three.
Silt	soil particles which are larger than clay and smaller than sand.
Spit	the length of a spade.
Succession	the availability of a crop over a long period.
Tilth	the crumb structure on the soil surface.
Trace element	a chemical which plants require in very small amounts.
Virus	an extremely small organism which can only exist in living things. It causes diseases in plants and animals.
Water stress	reduction in plant growth caused by too little water.

REFERENCES

The following items are available from
E. W. King & Co. Ltd
Monks Farm,
Kelvedon,
Essex CO5 9PG

Tel: 01376 570000

Seeds – Vegetables – an excellent range. Herb seeds – all 45 common herbs. Flower seeds - extensive list. Sweet peas - a Kings speciality.
Sundries – Cloches, Compost makers, Horticultural fleece, Labels, Organic Fertilisers, pH meters, Phostrogen products – a full range Secateurs Stakes

Weed killers. Biological Pest Control Organisms
Defenders Ltd
PO Box 131
Wye
Ashford
Kent
TN25 5TQ

Tel: 01233 813121

Fertilisers
Garden Direct
Geddings Road
Hoddesdon
Herts EN11 0LR

Tel: 01992 441888

Horticultural Fleece
Agralan
The Old Brickyard
Ashton Keynes
Swindon SN6 6QR

Tel: 01285 860015

Polytunnels
Solar Tunnels
2 Melrose Place
Ashington
W. Sussex RH20 3HH

Tel: 01903 742615

Ferryman Polytunnels
Unit C
The Old Creamery
Lapford
Crediton
Devon EX17 6AH

Tel: 01363 83444

First Tunnels
63 Dixon Street
Barrowford
Lancashire
BB9 8PL

Tel: 01282 601253

Fordingbridge Ltd
Arundel Road
Fontwell Arundel
West Sussex BN18 0SD

Tel: 01243 554455

Traditional Garden Equipment
Traditional Supply Co Ltd
Unit 12
Hewitts Industrial Estate
Elmbridge Road
Cranleigh
Surrey
GU6 8LW

Tel: 01483 273366

Reference Books

The Plant Finder

Lists over 65,000 plants, from alpines to trees and where to obtain them. The lay gardener's 'bible', updated annually. A comprehensive section on plant names.

The Vegetable Finder

Compiled by the Henry Doubleday Research Association. Lists sources of all commercially available vegetable varieties.

Robinsons Greenhouse Gardening.

Bernard Salt.

A no-nonsense practical guide for all gardeners – a vital source of information for both the novice and the more experienced gardener. (*Published by MPC*).

All of these titles are distributed by MPC.

INDEX

SECOND FOLD

Please

affix

stamp

E . W. King & Co. Ltd.,
Monks Farm,
Pantlings Lane,
Coggeshall Road,
KELVEDON
Essex
CO5 9PG

THIRD FOLD
TUCK INTO SECOND
FOLD

FIRST FOLD

E. W. King & Co. Ltd.,
Monks Farm,
Pantlings Lane,
Coggeshall Road,
Kelvedon,
Essex
C05 9PG

Please send me my FREE £5 seed voucher and a copy of KING'S seed catalogue.

Signed...

PLEASE USE BLOCK CAPITALS

Name...

Address..

....Post Code...........................